CW00345353

"Soft skills are absolutely critical to n
parents make the mistake that becau
that they will reach unprecedentec
underestimate the importance of em
skills that will get them there.

Peace is on to a winner here with this insightful book. It is great to see that she has written this book covering some of the ideas she shared with me (approximately 20 years ago), when she started to become aware of the importance of interpersonal skills as a means of achieving success in life and in the corporate world.

This is a must-read for all ages who want to be successful in their interpersonal relationships on their way to business and leadership success."

Mrs A. D'Almeida,
Pastor, Author, Social Entrepreneur and Director of Administration.

"Congratulations and very well done on writing this magnificent piece – truly practical and very comprehensive! A must-read for all parents. I learnt so much from reviewing the manuscript. A lot of time, thought, effort, hard work and diligence must have gone into this.

I love that the illustrations are evidence-based from respected and irrefutable sources, which gives credibility to the assertions. I found the approach very balanced, with lots of practical tips and detailed guidelines around implementation which adds value to the book as it's not just theoretical.

The use of summaries at the end of each chapter combined with the personal examples is in itself innovative for this type of book. It will encourage the reader."

Mr A. Odunsi
Minister, Management Consultant and Businessman

"As a former primary school teacher with many years' experience, I found this book very interesting and have enjoyed editing it."

Mrs J. Hoyle
Education Professional

Nurturing
Soft Skills

A Practical Guide for Developing Leadership
and Financial Literacy Skills in Children

Peace E. Ani

Matador
9 Priory Business Park,
Wistow Road, Kibworth Beauchamp,
Leicestershire. LE8 0RX
Tel: 0116 279 2299
Email: books@troubador.co.uk
Web: www.troubador.co.uk/matador
Twitter: @matadorbooks

ISBN 978 1800461 635

British Library Cataloguing in Publication Data.
A catalogue record for this book is available from the British Library.

Printed and bound in the UK by TJ Books Limited, Padstow, Cornwall
Typeset in 11pt Ten Oldstyle by Troubador Publishing Ltd, Leicester, UK

Matador is an imprint of Troubador Publishing Ltd

Dedicated to my children,
and all children for hope of a bright future.

*Train up a child in the way they should go: and when they are
old, they will not depart from it.*

Proverbs 22:6 (KJV)

About the Author

Peace E. Ani started her career in investment banking in the City after graduating with first class honours in BSc Mathematical Sciences in 2004. She is also the co-founder of Child Prodigy, a soft skills development workshop programme for children. Peace has over 16 years of professional experience within leading global institutions. She blogs for City Parents, where she has published several popular blogs.

As a senior professional and full-time working mother, she has a first-hand understanding of the challenges that new parents deal with trying to balance it all, as well as key insights into the skill sets that our children will need to develop early on to be more successful.

Peace has an MBA from Imperial College Business School and is also an Oxford University scholar where she completed a postgraduate degree in Strategy and Innovation. She holds a Fellow membership of the Chartered Management Institute (CMI), a chartered professional body in the UK, committed to the highest standards in management and leadership practice.

Peace believes in the unlimited potential in children with the right nurturing, and has a passion for inspiring young minds to maximise their potential. She is regularly called upon to give keynote speeches and inspirational talks at seminars, school events and conferences.

Contents

PART I
NURTURING A CHILD TO BE MORE CONFIDENT, OUTGOING, ARTICULATE, CREATIVE AND HAPPY

PART II
BRINGING IT ALL TOGETHER

Foreword

Although schools play a vital role in educating children, *Nurturing Soft Skills* focuses on the role parents need to play in equipping children with essential life skills. Lengthy COVID-19 lock-down periods, which have left some children without formal schooling for six months, have brought this into sharp focus.

Nurturing Soft Skills provides practical advice on how parents and guardians can use everyday activities to develop self-confidence and independent thinking skills in children. Peace Ani has carried out extensive research into approaches and theories on child development and introduces the COACH framework to facilitate the development of these skills in young children. This book skilfully demonstrates how parents can guide their children through a journey of self-discovery to become **C**onfident, **O**utgoing, **A**rticulate, **C**reative and **H**appy. Peace shares numerous examples from her own experience as a parent, and case studies based on her research, about how to develop leadership skills and enquiring minds in children.

Why is this important?

Today's children will be entering a globally competitive workforce where academic qualifications alone will not be enough. Employers are starting to place much more value on resilience, effective communication, self-motivation and confidence. This was confirmed in research conducted by the Sutton Trust in 2017, where 94% of employers surveyed indicated that life skills, including communication and teamwork, are as or more important than academic qualifications in the workplace.

Parents will learn the importance of playing an active and critical role in the development of their children, with tools and tips on how to lay the right foundation to nurture confident, creative and inquisitive minds; skills that will be of use throughout education, work and life.

Alice Sterling Honig, PhD, a professor in Child Development, and a licensed psychologist, averred, *"Family is the first school for young children, and parents are powerful models."*

If you think the responsibility to educate your child sits in schools, this book will challenge you to think again!

Teresa Esan, MBE
Education Consultant and Career Coach

Introduction

"Leadership and learning are indispensable to each other."

John F. Kennedy

In today's world of technological and social media advancement, the world is described as a 'global village' – a single community closely connected by information technology, with distance rapidly reduced by electronic social media. The term 'global village', coined by the Canadian media theorist Marshall McLuhan, was popularised in his book *Understanding Media* (1964). McLuhan described how technology has contracted the globe into a village due to the instantaneous movement of information. The use of technology has resulted in positive progress for society, in terms of people having the ability to reach out and transcend their neighbourhoods. This has resulted in increased communication between acquaintances, friends and families through social media, which may not have been possible otherwise. However, the digital age also has implications for forming new social norms, and the sociological implications of the 'global village' are yet to be fully realised.

Borrowing the term 'village' and its conceptual meaning, I am going to leap to another instance where a similar idea, albeit within a different context, forms the basis for this book.

The old saying 'it takes a village to raise a child' is still relevant today. This conceptual village can include: parents, teachers, mentors, sports coaches, music teachers, swimming instructors, private tutors, Sunday school teachers, friends' parents, grandparents, aunts and uncles, nannies, *au pairs*, childminders, doctors and nurses, neighbours, TV or, dare I say it, social media. The various individuals or elements that make up the cohort of our customised 'village' sometimes act as an oversight or engagement tool. In some instances, the individuals involved go beyond their professional capacity, demonstrated by the advice they offer, keeping an eye on the children on behalf of the parents, reinforcing discipline or reporting any unusual goings-on in the neighbourhood. Essentially, this 'village' is composed of people or tools that contribute to a child's well-being, learning and development in one way or another. This includes anyone who has pointed out an undesirable behaviour in a child, exposed them to enriching experiences, offered babysitting services or helped to support the parents in any way. Fundamentally, for a child to maximise their potential, it takes more than the parents being fully engaged and playing their role as best as possible. This is especially true in situations with different family dynamics from the traditional setup, or where the parents have to rely on external support for some elements of their childcare and the child's development.

Typically, parents taking an interest in good child-rearing and education want their children to be happy, courageous, authentic individuals who flourish in their endeavours, and do better than they have. Most parents want their children to be successful – to aspire and one day inspire, while getting the most out of life. However, success in this area can mean different things depending on the circumstances and phase of life. Success can mean: a fun and memorable childhood; good SATs or eleven-plus secondary school common entrance exam result; raising conscientious, kind and empathetic children; or for your child to have the analytic prowess to escape the grasp of superstition and fake news. Therefore, success in applying the best practices is of course relative and defined by different idiosyncratic measures.

In my personal experience, I find that some people, who measure success by how much money they have in the bank account, find they are still lacking something and are still not happy when they get the money they thought was all they needed. We all want to be successful and maximise our potential, but in my opinion, success should be measured by influence and positive impact on society. Therefore, as parents and caretakers, our children's journey is in our hands to some extent. This is because we have the responsibility to start them off, through teaching and modelling the skill sets and behaviours that they will need for a fulfilling life experience. As they lead themselves and others into a future world where the only certainty is change, parents have the first opportunity to either set their children up well – or let the status quo decide their future.

Whilst this is not a responsibility to be taken lightly, the beauty of it is that the little things we do every day can make such a big difference in the long term, in nurturing and supporting children to maximise their potential.

Nurturing Soft Skills is a guide for developing soft skills, specifically authentic leadership, and financial literacy as a key area of competency in children. Leadership is a term used frequently in politics, business or corporate environments, as employers typically seek employees who can successfully interact with other colleagues and clients. A good leader requires a number of soft skills to be successful, and some of the concepts discussed in this book could be relevant for professional and leadership development. The difference between soft and hard skills is defined and discussed in Chapter 1.

Nurturing Soft Skills sets out the early leadership predictors and serves as a useful toolkit for parents, or child development practitioners, to consciously nurture children to develop key life skills early on. This book is largely for parents with primary school-aged children, as these are the foundational years. In some instances, children's developmental trajectories are set early on; teachers and caretakers group the children based on their perceived ability. Quieter children, who lack the necessary confidence to demonstrate what they know, risk being placed in lower ability groups and remaining there. Confident and more outgoing children, who are not afraid to put up their hands, often get more recognition, and will, in all likelihood, thereby be grouped higher.

We are parents who want to do the best as custodians, but sometimes due to competing demands on our time and life pressures, we may not be aware of the best practices for nurturing our children to develop the key skill sets of life.

Why I wrote this book

I became interested in sourcing best practices when I was expecting my first child, and even more so when I came across the following quotation:

> "The goal of education is not to increase the amount of knowledge but to create the possibilities for a child to invent and discover, to create [individuals] who are capable of doing new things."
>
> Jean Piaget

The premise of this book is based on the above quotation and as ascribed in Figure 1. Jean Piaget, the Swiss developmental psychologist and philosopher known for his child cognitive development studies, believed that cognitive development is progressive and subject to both biological maturation and environmental experiences. His theory was derived from the idea that children construct an understanding of the world around them, through adjusting the discrepancy between what they discover against what they already know. The stages of intellectual development formulated by Piaget are related to major developments in brain growth. It is important to note that the periods presented are averages, and some children may achieve various developmental milestones earlier or later but still be within the normal range.

The guidelines discussed in this book are mostly targeted at children aged three to 11, the pre-operational and concrete operational stages, according to Piaget's theory of cognitive development, as set out in Table 1:

Typical Age Range	Description of Stage	Developmental Phenomena
Birth to nearly 2 years	*Sensorimotor* Experiencing the world through senses and actions (looking, touching, mouthing)	Object permanence Stranger anxiety
2 to 6 years	*Pre-operational* Representing things with words and images but lacking logical reasoning	Pretend play Egocentrism Language development
7 to 11 years	*Concrete operational* Thinking logically about concrete events; grasping concrete analogies and performing arithmetical operations	Conservation Mathematical transformations
12 through adulthood	*Formal operational* Abstract reasoning	Abstract logic Potential for moral reasoning

Table 1: Piaget's Theory of Cognitive Development

By the pre-operational stage, between two to six years old, children begin to use language and are egocentric, only seeing things from their viewpoints. During the concrete operational stage, between seven and 11 years old, children can think more logically, classify and sort objects in order or by several features. By the age of 12, this becomes more advanced and they become more concerned with the hypothetical and the future, able to create hypotheses and tests.

I have spent over a decade researching this topic and believe other parents will also find this information useful in supporting their child or children to identify and maximise their potential.

This book covers such useful information on how to encourage confident, healthy, happy, charismatic and creative children. I believe these key qualities are appropriate for all children. It's fair to assume that most, if not all, parents will want the best for their children. Teachers and future potential employers may also have an interest in helping to encourage such rounded leadership qualities in developing personalities early on.

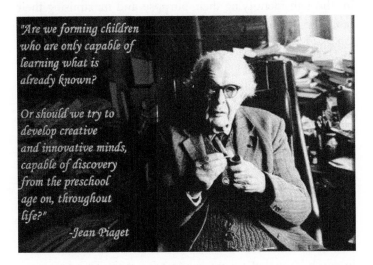

"Are we forming children who are only capable of learning what is already known?

Or should we try to develop creative and innovative minds, capable of discovery from the preschool age on, throughout life?"

-Jean Piaget

Figure 1: Jean Piaget, child cognitive development psychologist

In *Nurturing Soft Skills,* I have defined a simple and effective framework, called COACH, which stands for nurturing a child to be more:

Confident
Outgoing
Articulate
Creative
Happy.

As parents we have the responsibility to create a nurturing and loving environment for our children to thrive, be happy, feel loved and feel accepted in. However, there is also the other side of supporting and coaching our children to make something of themselves and improve the society they live in, through identifying their purpose and maximising their potential. I should add that this book addresses both points by helping parents develop a strategy for their child development objectives. By applying the framework set out in this book, you, the parent, will not only develop a leadership mind-set in your children but maybe also in yourself. The theories and best practices presented will complement existing approaches from a parent or professional practitioner perspective. I find that I learn a lot through and from my children. This learning is not limited to new things, a refresher on early physics or proper grammar, but also increased self-awareness. Through teaching our children, we become more refined and continue to improve. For example, when I observe certain behaviours in my children that are not so attractive, it gives me a moment to self-reflect. Through correcting the undesirable behaviours in our children, the increased self-awareness helps us to improve on some of our own less desirable behaviours. Over time, I have found that I am learning to become a better person and am more self-aware, through trying to lead by example.

The objective of this book is to help like-minded parents identify and develop the soft skills their child or children will need in the future, through nurture, exposure, aspirations, resilience and motivation. For example, teaching children not to be afraid to try something just because they think they might fail. Instead, they should see failure as a sign of aiming high and it means they have tried. The key is to embrace the concept of 'failing forward' whenever our children, or we, experience any setbacks. 'Failing forward' is a term popularised by John C. Maxwell, an internationally recognised leadership expert, speaker and author who has sold over 16 million books. The definition of 'failing forward' is best described by the following quotation from Maxwell:

"The essence of man is imperfection. Know that you're going to make mistakes. The fellow who never makes a mistake takes his orders from one who does. Wake up and realise this: Failure is simply a price we pay to achieve success."

I will add that failure can sometimes be a gift, a process for developing empathy, character and increased expertise. I believe that one of the drawbacks of children always winning and getting their way is the lost opportunity to develop character, a sense of reality and empathy. Therefore, if you are looking for a book about how to ensure your child always wins throughout life, I'm afraid this is not it. This book is about getting the balance right to ensure there are more well-rounded children with high leadership potential.

I believe that a significant proportion of the problems in society today could be solved by getting things right at home from early on. This is well summarised by the following quotation from Kathleen Strottman, the Executive Director at the Congressional Coalition on Adoption Institute in the United States:

"Strong families build strong communities, and strong communities build strong villages, and strong villages build strong nations."

From personal experience, over my career I have observed first-hand that children who were nurtured consciously, according to most of the concepts being discussed in this book, outperform their peers later on. Success is not measured by academic achievement alone, with increasing emphasis on soft skills. Environmental factors play a big part in nurturing children. An article published by *The Guardian* newspaper in 2017 about the United Kingdom's leading elite found that Oxford University graduates in philosophy, politics and economics (PPE) represent a significant proportion. Generations have reproduced after themselves, due to the harnessing of social networks over time from early nurturing practices. This, in my opinion, also suggests that there is something about the early nurture that enables the students to later thrive in the environment at leading institutions that have churned out a significant portion of world-changers and leaders.

In the early part of my career, I realised that I could have ascended the career ladder more swiftly if I had demonstrated the full range of soft skill sets captured within the COACH framework. With time, however, I developed some of these skills and eventually caught up, but it was the hard way. The point of this book is to set out the easy way from what I have learnt as a result of some of my shortcomings and my subsequent extensive research. There is a Chinese proverb which states that learning from each other is better than learning by yourself.

Strategic thinking

When it comes to planning, there are those who may have planned the next five years, while others have followed the strategy of 'just go with the flow and see what happens' – which in some circumstances has worked for this group of people. However, there are some things in life that you just should not leave to chance. Raising children is a long-term commitment and you may not see the impact of your actions for decades. As a result, some parents prioritise things that lead to immediate impact such as promotions at work. Even with the best intentions they slowly reorganise their priorities but are then surprised when they do not get the desired outcome with their children. That is because, according to Clayton Christensen, author and former Harvard Business School professor, strategy, whether in companies or in life, is created over time through the hundreds of everyday decisions about how and what you spend your time on. No matter how well you articulate your purpose and strategy for your life, what matters is the cumulative impact of your everyday actions. It means sometimes boundaries have to be set – friends and families cannot make it a habit to just turn up or call you at any time of the day. You have to be consistent and reinforce the boundaries when necessary. It is also not about having excessive resources for a strategy to be effective. It is more about being consistent. In fact, from some case studies I came across while completing my MBA, limited resources can be a blessing, as sometimes having too many resources could lead to failure if not managed efficiently. This is not to say abundant resources lead to failure, but rather that limited resources are not necessarily a hindrance or reason for failure, and they don't preclude you from being able to apply and use the best practices in this book effectively.

How to use this book

There is no 'one size fits all' toolkit that anyone can share with you that will lead to the desired outcomes for your child or children. This is because children are wired differently – even identical twins; the hot water that softens the potatoes hardens the egg. However, I have set out a framework that a representative sample of parents have followed successfully with example case studies from numerous families who have shared their best practices. This framework of best practices is in effect a prediction of what outcomes we may achieve because of the cumulative impact of the small actions or decisions we make about our children every day. In *Nurturing Soft Skills*, I have summarised some of the key insights and recommended best practices – from both a first- and second-hand basis.

It is my hope that this book will contribute towards preventing and solving some pockets of the problems in our society today, where the root cause is in the paucity or absence of family dynamics and early nurturing.

Perspectives referenced

The perspectives from four consecutive generations are explored – covering the baby boomer generation born between 1949 and 1959, generation X, millennials born after 1982 and generation Z. This book is most relevant for those that fall into the last three categories, and their children who represent the next generation and beyond. This book covers perspectives from families with different religious backgrounds and beliefs, single-parent and two-parent families. The common factor is that all are united in the goal of helping children maximise their potential. Parents with children who are now into their twenties and early thirties at the time of writing, contributed to the focus group discussions to analyse how applying the theories and best practices explored in this book resulted in the desired outcome. For completeness, the adult children of some of these parents were also interviewed to capture their perspectives and opinions about how much of a role their parents' approach played in how they have turned out. Aliases such as Meghan, Rose and Mark are used. Personal information and stories provide a helpful context. The range and breadth of the stories should resonate with most, and therefore make the best practices relevant and applicable. Additionally, depending on your child's inherent strengths, they may not need support with all the skills discussed in this book. I would still encourage you to read the entire book in order to maximise the benefits therein, as there are overlaps and correlations between some of the skills. Following which, you could just dip in and out of the specific chapters to focus on key areas. Although it appears on the whole that a lot of the advice in this book centres around structure, keeping children busy and engaged, this is intentional to some extent. I remember having a conversation with a friend's 12-year-old son, Jay Murray, at a family gathering, as he had come home for the weekend from his public boarding school. Over the conversation, I was surprised to learn how the students from his school had scheduled activities, through the day and on weekends, designed to keep them occupied.

As one of the many variants of the proverb '*the devil makes work for idle hands to do*' – people who have nothing worthwhile to do or think about may think of something bad to do. This is an old idea dating back as far as the fourth century from theologian St. Jerome. As one of the oldest expressions in the English language, Jerome's version was '*... do something, so that the devil always finds you occupied*'. We see the consequences of this reflected in some of the unfortunate events in society today, where many young people have gotten themselves into trouble or into compromising situations due to idleness, lack of scheduled activities or limited access to amenities to keep them engaged. However, for balance and in the right context, I believe that incorporating leisure time or some quiet idle time to meditate, think and refocus can lead to increased productivity.

Theories and practices

The concepts discussed could be considered theories and suppositions. Theories are valuable because they can help to explain or predict what will happen before you experience it. The point of this book is to apply theories and practices today to help nurture our children to achieve their potential for their own good, and for a better future for society.

Children do not come with a manual and this is not an attempt to create one. This is a guide for parents or child development practitioners who want to apply some of the theories and best practices early on. As with any theory, there will be outliers and sometimes correlation does not necessarily equate to causation. Clayton Christensen, former Harvard Business School professor and author of *How Will You Measure Your Life?*, provides a good definition of what a theory is. Using the analogy of flight, Christensen states that wings do not make birds fly; if they did, chickens would have mastered flight. The law of aerodynamics, according to NASA, describes the way air moves around things to cause flight. The rules of aerodynamics explain how an aeroplane is able to fly, as anything that moves through air reacts to the forces of aerodynamics. These forces of flight are lift, weight, thrust and drag. The forces make an object move up and down, and faster or slower. How much of each force there is changes how the object moves through the air. One of the forces, drag, can be likened to the default forces and distractions that our children are exposed to: a force that tries to drag something down and makes it hard to make progress. In contrast, thrust is the force that is the opposite of drag. Thrust is the push that moves something forward. Therefore, for an aircraft to keep moving forward, it must have more thrust than drag.

This book serves to provide additional thrust in the form of best practices for developing soft skills. I believe that by sharing some case study examples of early failures and successes, more parents will find the content of this book a useful source of thrust for developing soft skills in their children. This book is written in the first person – my voice as the author – and I share stories and examples synthesised from various sources. The intention is to sharpen the reader's awareness in nurturing soft skills in their children, in themselves and to lead to improved family dynamics.

PART I

Nurturing a child to be more:
Confident
Outgoing
Articulate
Creative
Happy

CHAPTER 1

Hard Skills versus Soft Skills

*"The most dangerous leadership myth is that leaders are born
– that there is a genetic factor to leadership. This myth asserts
that people simply either have certain charismatic qualities or
not. That is nonsense: in fact, the opposite is true. Leaders are
made rather than born."*

Warren Bennis

American scholar, pioneer of leadership studies and author

Hard skills are specific and measurable academic and
technical abilities such as writing, maths, reading and the
ability to use software programs. Typically, hard skills are
taught in the classroom through books or training materials
on the job. Financial literacy, which we cover in Chapter 7,
is typically considered a hard skill. However, this has been
added because it is relevant for completeness as it is a much-
needed skill for children to develop in a world of growing
debt issues and addictive over-spending. Through my

research into the primary school curriculum while writing this book, I found that financial management is missing in most educational curricula.

Contrastingly, soft skills are subjective, less tangible and harder to quantify, such as etiquette, getting along with others, resilience, behaviours, listening and engaging in small talk. Soft skills are also known as 'people skills' or 'interpersonal skills', and describes the way one interacts with people. Other examples of soft skills are motivation, patience, persuasion, teamwork, time management and a good work ethic. Leadership is also an example of a soft skill which encompasses a number of other soft skills and qualities such as integrity, authenticity, confidence, communication, collaboration, flexibility, problem-solving abilities, positivity, creativity, commitment, responsibility and the ability to delegate. Additionally, the most sought-after candidates for leadership roles are those with a high degree of emotional intelligence, which describes the ability to relate well with people and get the best outcomes, also referred to as the emotional quotient (EQ).

I first came across the concept of emotional intelligence approximately 20 years ago, from a classmate at university reading the international bestseller *Emotional Intelligence* by Daniel Goleman. I was intrigued by the subtitle, '*How EQ matters more than IQ*'. This was the first time I had come across such a concept. IQ (intelligence quotient) was the main differentiator I had been aware of at the time and, as such, most people I knew aspired to having high IQs, especially within my university cohort. Perhaps it was because, when a group of mathematicians comes together to socialise, it is only a matter of time before we start comparing scores from our last IQ tests. We all naively believed at the time that the higher your IQ score, the higher your chances of success. While not false, the reality is more nuanced.

Emotional quotient was originally defined as a measure of the ability of an individual to recognise, understand and empathise with how people, including oneself, are feeling. Evidence shows that people with higher emotional intelligence know and manage their own feelings well, as well as read and deal with other people's feelings effectively. This gives them an advantage in any domain of life. The term was coined in a 1990 research paper by two psychology professors, John D. Mayer of the University of New Hampshire (UNH) and Peter Salovey of Yale. However, in a book by Steven J. Stein, PhD and Howard E. Book, MD called *The EQ Edge*, they define EQ as:

"The set of skills that enable us to make our way in a complex world – the personal, social and survival aspects of overall intelligence, the elusive common sense and sensitivity that are essential to effective daily functioning. It has to do with the ability to read the political and social environment, and landscape to intuitively grasp what others want and need, what strengths, and weaknesses are; to remain unruffled by stress; and to be engaging. The kind of person others want to be around and will follow."

According to Goleman, *'Human competencies like self-awareness, self-regulation, and empathy add value to cognitive abilities in many domains of life, from workplace effectiveness and leadership to health and relationships.'* The opportunity to develop emotional

5

intelligence starts in the earliest years, though the capacity continues to form throughout the school years. According to Goleman, the first three or four years of life are a period when the brain grows to almost two thirds its whole size, evolving at a more rapid rate than it ever will again, and emotional learning is the foremost taking place at this stage.

After reading Daniel Goleman's *Emotional Intelligence*, I experienced a mind-set shift. There are a number of stories shared in the book which perhaps best illustrate this shift and the perceived benefits of this phenomenon called 'Emotional Intelligence'. I learnt that small tweaks in our perspectives and the way we respond to situations could yield opposite and better results.

The first story I want to share from the book is about a potential road-rage scenario. Goleman suggests that, instead of being irritated and annoyed by what appears to be dangerous driving by another driver who cuts dangerously close to you as you're driving, to instead consider various scenarios and rationale for the dangerous driving. A line of thought such as the driver trying to get to the hospital for a medical emergency means we would be more understanding of the circumstances that are contributing to their dangerous driving. In essence, we are more likely to temper anger with mercy and have a more measured response just by considering different perspectives and short-circuiting the build-up of rage. In essence, reframing a situation more positively diffuses anger. The second story was about a married couple. A situation that could have easily escalated out of control, potentially leading to divorce, was short-circuited through the application of emotional intelligence.

A spouse choosing to show some empathy towards the other about what a challenging day the other may have had, and suggesting they go out for a meal for date night to discuss each other's day, diffused what appeared to be mounting tension. This approach dissolved any chance of the issue escalating, and there was harmony.

As illustrated by these stories, emotional intelligence is that 'special something' that is intangible and affects the way we manage behaviour and make decisions leading to positive outcomes. Travis Bradberry, author of *Emotional Intelligence 2.0*, defines emotional intelligence as the ability to navigate social complexities and make personal decisions that yield positive results. Emotional intelligence is the capacity to be aware of, control and express one's emotions, and to handle interpersonal relationships wisely and empathetically.

Bradberry asserts that children learn emotional intelligence from their parents; they *"absorb behaviours through watching their parents every day. Children are like a sponge, attuned to their parents' emotional awareness and behaviour".*

EQ is therefore described as one of the biggest drivers of leadership success. A study published in *Forbes* magazine in 2014 found that 90% of top-performing leaders have high EQs. Another study by TalentSmart, a provider of emotional intelligence training, found that children who develop a high level of emotional intelligence carry these skills into adulthood, which gives them a leg-up in leadership and in life.

This chapter sets out the importance of nurturing soft skills in children because:

• soft skills increase the value of hard skills

- soft skills development is progressive and can be subject to environmental influences
- getting along with people and displaying a positive attitude are important and contribute to positive relationships and outcomes in general
- children's development and capability trajectory are set early on based on perception, and less confident children could be incorrectly streamed.

According to Carol Carter, author, public speaker and leadership and communications coach – 'soft skills can promote competence and employability'. Traditionally, schools prioritise the value of 'hard' (academic) skills, but the impacts of the loss of opportunity to develop soft skills have played out and continue to play out in society today. From my professional experience, I have found that employers place equal or more emphasis on soft skills such as effective communication, teamwork, critical thinking, problem solving and innovation. In most leading organisations, these are among some of the most sought-after skills.

Primary school children are generally not expected to possess soft skills; however, this can be a lost opportunity to nurture these skills that contribute to better life satisfaction at a key development stage. Having emotionally intelligent parents is itself an enormous benefit to the child. The little things those of us who are parents consciously do or don't do daily with our children, start to lay the foundation for their future temperament, character and behaviours. The key is to do things with good measure and balance, such that it's not overbearing on the child. Additionally, forty years of Stanford research, titled *The Marshmallow Experiment*, suggests that primary school age is not too early for children to start to develop key soft skills. The details of this Stanford research, which provided a key early insight into children's developing qualities from the age of four or five, is discussed in more detail in Chapter 7.

Furthermore, the World Economic Forum (WEF), an independent, impartial and not-for-profit international organisation, headquartered in Switzerland and committed to improving society, has set out the critical skills and knowledge that people will need the most to thrive from 2020 onwards compared to 2015. These have been defined by engaging political, business and other leaders of society who shape global and industry agendas.

With the appropriate nurturing from an early age, children have the opportunity to develop and master these key life skills. The table below shows the top ten skills that were critical in 2015 according to the research by the WEF, and the shift between such desired skills, from 2015 to 2020 and beyond.

No.	Important life skills in 2015	Important life skills in 2020 and beyond	Skills to develop by 2030
1	Complex problem solving	Complex problem solving	Creativity
2	Coordinating with others	Critical thinking	Complex problem solving
3	People management	Creativity	Coordinating with others
4	Critical thinking	People management	Critical thinking

No.	Important life skills in 2015	Important life skills in 2020 and beyond	Skills to develop by 2030
5	Negotiation	Coordinating with others	Judgement and decision making
6	Quality control	Emotional intelligence	People management
7	Service orientation	Judgement and decision making	Service orientation
8	Judgement and decision making	Service orientation	Emotional intelligence
9	Active listening	Negotiation	Negotiation
10	Creativity	Cognitive flexibility	Cognitive flexibility

Table 2: WEF's top 10 skills
Source: World Economic Forum

As can be seen from the table, and with the prevalence of artificial intelligence (AI), the importance of skills like creativity will become even more important in the future, and the ability for complex problem solving will remain sought after. As the world fills with more sophisticated AI and ubiquitous technology, soft skills will define the competitive edge. According to Ryan Jenkins writing for *Inc.*, those interested in thriving in the high-tech world developing around us need emotional intelligence and soft skills.

Soft skills represent the top three missing skills of job applicants, according to the Society of Human Resource Management's (SHRM) '*2019 State of the Workplace*' survey. The significance of developing and applying social and emotional skills is growing. Fifty-seven per cent of leaders say soft skills are more important than hard skills. Employers aren't looking for the same level of deep knowledge and technical skill as they did in the past, as 40% of employers believe artificial intelligence will help fill the skills gap. Therefore, as part of the fourth industrial revolution (4IR) powered by digital transformation, the prevalence of AI will only make soft skills more necessary and valuable because they are the skills robots can't yet automate. Furthermore, soft skills are more transferable across careers and industries. This is discussed in more detail in Chapter 10 about future proofing.

These important future skills are covered by the COACH framework.

The COACH framework

The next five chapters cover the importance of each of the skills represented by the acronym COACH, namely: Confident, Outgoing, Articulate, Creative and Happy. Each chapter offers simple everyday ways to nurture these skills, drawing on real-life case studies. These skills have been mapped to the top ten skills set out by the World Economic Forum to help parents ensure these are covered in everyday interactions. See Figure 2.

As can be seen from the mapping, there are some overlaps. For example, a person with healthy confidence may generally have good people management and negotiation skills, and is likely to coordinate well with others. Similarly, an outgoing or charismatic individual may typically have a high level of emotional intelligence. A creative person may use their creativity to break down and solve problems, applying some cognitive flexibility, and so on.

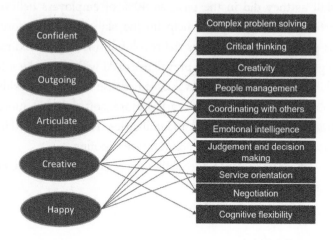

Figure 2: Mapping of the top ten skills to the COACH framework

However, while there is more emphasis in schools for students to develop hard skills from learning STEM subjects (Science, Technology, Engineering and Mathematics) to prepare students for future success, the impact of these soft skills should not be underestimated. Lisa Phillips, author of *The Artistic Edge: 7 Skills Children Need to Succeed in an Increasingly Right Brain World*, highlights the importance of the 'arts', in helping to develop some of these soft skills. Phillips asserts that creativity, confidence and problem solving are some of the transferable skills that she acquired through the arts and playing sports. This is covered in more detail in Chapter 5: Creative. For example, there are significant overlaps between the daily routine of a gymnast or a football player, which could contribute to their school or future career success, such as the confidence gained from the discipline, repeated practice, consistency, persistence and being goal-oriented.

A key takeaway from this is that these critical soft skills are not necessarily inherited but can be learnt and developed over time.

SUMMARY: SOFT SKILLS DEVELOPMENT

- Cognitive development is progressive and can be subject to environmental influences.
- Children's development and capability trajectory can be set early on based on perception.
- Less confident children could be incorrectly ranked.
- Soft skills can improve competence and performance, as defined by the acronym COACH:

   Confident – confidence leads to better performance
   Outgoing – charisma and likeability are fundamental to success, as they open doors and attract favours
   Articulate – better communicators generally excel
   Creative – creativity boosts innovation, which leads to a competitive advantage and sustainable success
   Happy – a great attitude is essential as people generally like people with a positive attitude

CHAPTER 2

Confident

"A strong leader avoids becoming overconfident to the point of impaired judgement."

Daniel Lubetzky
Businessman, founder of Kind Bar

Confidence is critical in ensuring that we deliver a message convincingly. Performing confidently before an audience is a critical skill that sets leaders apart from the rest. According to author Lisa Phillips, through theatre performances children practise stepping out of their comfort zone as this process gives them the confidence to perform in front of large audiences. Other practical ways in which parents can increase their children's confidence are set out below.

1 – Allocating early responsibilities

Giving children responsibilities from an early age helps to build their self-esteem and confidence. For example, simple early responsibilities from the age of three, such as making their beds, can go a long way. By the age of six my children could sort their laundry into light- and dark-coloured piles; by age eight they could set the washing machine for the child load and hang out their washing once done. However, that does not necessarily imply it should be their sole responsibility at that age, although the occasional completion of these chores would not be overbearing. For example, my children all make their beds most mornings without a reminder. They take turns to sort the laundry, although sometimes they need a reminder. The key is balance alongside these responsibilities, to ensure that children also have fun around the house as well as going out to explore and learn about life around them.

Despite it being known that children are creatures of habit, parents do not usually think about allocating responsibilities from a young age. This may be because of an inherent expectation about the age at which we think children can be responsible. I believe, as parents, that we can help our children become more capable by showing and supporting them early on. This is an old principle and supported from the Book of Proverbs in the Bible. While I understand that not all readers refer to the Bible as a reference point for raising their children, nonetheless, the concept is broadly applicable to the context of this book. Proverbs, chapter 22, verse six translates as:

"Train and start children off on the way they should go, and even when they are old they will not turn from it."

I share this not just as a Christian but because the principle from this excerpt also correlates with Piaget's theory about the defining years of childhood development. Once this is set properly early on, with the key skill set, it should ensure a solid foundation for happier, healthier and more positive outcomes in adulthood.

Several best practices suggest that giving children responsibilities from early on not only helps them build confidence and self-esteem but also gives them a sense of responsibility and knowledge that they are contributing to society. There is a list of different age-appropriate responsibilities for pre-school and primary school-aged children from parenting expert Cara Sue Achterberg in the additional resources section at the end of this book.

From our case study characters, Rose, who is now in her mid to late twenties, recalls having some responsibilities from a primary school age. She shares a story of being given some money to go to the local convenience shop, which involved getting on the bus to travel a couple of stops when she was in Year Six (aged ten). She recalls having a pound coin and that there was to be some change brought back. The experience helped Rose develop more confidence.

As part of the focus group discussion, it was interesting to see different perspectives from other participants about the impact of birth order when it came to early responsibility. In Rose's case, she was also incidentally the first-born and therefore, by default, had some oversight responsibilities to her younger siblings. Another participant, let us call him Mark, stated that because he was the third-born, he felt he was not as confident as his older siblings were; he perceived they were given real responsibilities. Mark, who by any standard could be considered an overachiever (a top 100 graduate in the UK from the University of Oxford), recognised for his innovative entrepreneurial visions, states that as the third-born of four children, and a second son, "I *didn't feel significant.*" This was because he wasn't the first-born son, nor was he the last-born child, who can be considered to be the parents' pet or the cutest, in his opinion. Additionally, he felt that the responsibilities a third-born had were very different to what the first-born would have, in terms of complexity and usefulness. However, Mark explains that eventually his confidence at home developed and came from being given some responsibilities for things that were useful for other people.

It was also interesting to find that Mark felt that his youngest sibling, being the last-born, was even less confident, and he attributed this to the sibling not having key responsibilities at home compared to the older siblings. He went on to suggest that he believed that had the situation been reversed, with the last-born being the first-born, the dynamic and her level of confidence would have been different. "*She would have been a lot more confident,*" he says. Awareness of this potential impact of sibling order dynamics may ensure that parents factor this in as they manage the family situation for the optimal outcome. Through my research, although anecdotal in this instance, I found that when older siblings left home to go to university or otherwise, this sometimes created an opportunity for the younger siblings to step up to take on more responsibilities and therefore develop their confidence.

The role of the parents in these situations and the subconscious biases towards different children is critical, and parents should ensure they make a conscious effort to manage this better. At the same time, on the contrary, there are examples of first-born children who develop insecurities because of the parents' approach and possibly unrealistically high expectations of them. From personal experience, I found out that our eldest child temporarily developed some early resentment because of some of the high expectations we had of her. As a very capable and conscientious child, we had inadvertently developed an unhealthy dependency on her. With young children and my husband and me working full time in demanding roles, needless to say, sometimes we all felt the pressure. During one of our weekly discussions, my daughter highlighted that she felt that we were easier on the younger siblings, while we always seemed to expect more from her. She stated that sometimes she just wanted to be childish and goof around with her younger siblings, rather than having to be the serious, responsible one. This feedback was very useful as it improved our self-awareness. We immediately took steps to address this emerging issue so that we did not inadvertently contribute to sibling rivalry – through differences in our responses and expectations of our children. In line with this shift, emotional intelligence suggests that the key to getting the best out of anyone, whether as a parent, teacher or manager at work, is to understand the difference between people and adapting one's style.

Let me share another story about a family who decided to give their daughter some relatively straightforward responsibilities from around the age of five, which incidentally, the daughter took pride in. Let us call her Jane. For example, Jane could make her bed, sort the laundry, load the washing machine, and by age seven, she could dress up her one-year-old sibling. However, this all began unintentionally, partly due to her enthusiasm to help and out of curiosity. Over time, Jane advanced to being able to help her younger sibling with putting on his outdoor coat and shoes occasionally. In other instances, Jane sometimes helped to choose her younger sibling's outfit for the day. According to Jane's mother, by the time Jane was nine years old, she could change and fully dress her sibling. She would also volunteer to set the dinner table and tidy up afterwards. Taking ownership of these responsibilities had a positive effect and boosted Jane's confidence. Over time, the impact resulted in her taking the initiative to tutor her younger siblings during the holidays or at weekends, to the extent that she would prepare her teaching notes in advance, although in most cases this was done as part of their imaginative and fun role-playing. The resulting impact of this early responsibility is that Jane went on to be selected as Head Girl during her final year of primary school, and also secured a place at one of the leading secondary schools in the country.

Another example involves a friend who is a senior executive for a leading financial services organisation. She has two children, both under the age of ten. Let us call her Meghan. Her husband is an entrepreneur developing a Fintech (financial technology services) start-up. Meghan shares that her son and daughter had responsibilities from as early as possible. *"As soon as they could walk,"* she quips. Some of these responsibilities included putting toys away and taking used cups and bowls to the kitchen. From the age of five, they learnt to make their beds. Meghan explains that the chores did not have to be executed perfectly, but the key was just to help her children develop the mind-set of being responsible for something and contributing to the household chores.

Similarly, from the age of two, I encouraged my son to make his bed every morning – that way he started to understand the idea of tidying up his room, although he needed to be reminded almost every day. The point was not about making his bed perfectly initially but to develop the mind-set of having an early responsibility. With time, he could actually make his bed really well and took pride in it. By the time he was three and a half years old he took on the role of the 'bed-making officer', as he would check everyone had made their bed well most mornings, and would ask his older siblings to tuck in the corners if he thought it didn't look very straight. Although my husband and I found this hilarious, his older siblings didn't always see the funny side, understandably. On occasions, when I'm not pressed for time, I let him assist in folding his laundry and taking it to his room. He actually enjoys this and has also developed a sense of responsibility since completing these little chores from the age of two or three. This is important as children are creatures of habit and through learning about responsibilities and accountability, they're then likely to grow up to become responsible adults with a sense of accountability.

II – Identifying and developing expertise around a core talent

Large corporate organisations typically set annual objectives for employees' professional development, and to become known as a subject-matter expert (SME) in a particular activity or departmental responsibility. Developing these capabilities not only boosts confidence but also improves overall morale.

The same principle is applicable at home. In my experience with children, I've observed that being known for a special skill or knowledge contributes to boosting the child's confidence and gives them the opportunity to stand out. While it is impressive for people to generally be good at everything, through my research I found that just being good or average in everything has its limitations. Mark, the Oxford University PhD graduate from the focus group, states that from working for a leading management consultancy, he found that in order to make progress up the career ladder it was 'essential to be great and stand out for at least one skill'. Mark explains that in his opinion sometimes parents inadvertently contribute to eroding their child's confidence by expecting them to be great at everything, rather than nurturing them to discover their core talent.

From observing some of the leaders and influencers in society today, they all started off in one area – Bill Gates is known for computers; Warren Buffett for investments; Tiger Woods is known for golf; David Beckham for football; Michael Jordan for basketball; Beyoncé is known for music. Most of these influencers mastered their core talent which then created a platform that they leveraged for other initiatives and capabilities.

Mark further explains that his confidence came from being academically brilliant, as an Oxonian scholar and a subject-matter expert in medicine. He describes his family dynamic as a family of smart children and states that some parents may take their children's abilities for granted. In Mark's case he found that his parents never said 'well done'. There was no real acknowledgement or praise for winning prizes because it was expected. While he felt some resentment initially, over time he became more resilient. He stopped expecting his parents to appreciate his achievements, and instead channelled his effort through self-motivation to break new heights. However, a good takeaway from Mark's experience is that the key to helping children develop confidence and self-belief is to support them to find what they excel in and celebrate it. Celebrate children for their effort, achievements, abilities, talents and say 'well done'.

Avoid comparing children

The worry that comparisons can create insecurities and resentment between children, or even adults, is understandable. There will inevitably be different qualities in every child that we may place different value on, and therefore cause us to inadvertently compare our children which may negatively impact their confidence. For example, making statements about how one child is better in x, y or z is different to highlighting the different things that each child is good at. According to the old adage – it is not what you say but how you say it. I have found that it helps to say that your sister or brother is good at x and you are good at y; you should both help each other get better in the area you have specialist knowledge or ability in. Putting it that way is different to saying, "Your sibling is better at this – why can't you be more like him or her?"

Academic achievement-based confidence

From observation, I have found that in some parts of the world, academic achievement is celebrated as the pinnacle of success. Many parents make huge sacrifices in order to give their children the best opportunities they are aware of and are able to. Consequently, children with high academic ability from some of these communities appeared to be relatively confident within their family setup. However, this was not necessarily the case outside the family among their counterparts because they lacked the same level of soft skills that their counterparts excelled in, such as effective communication, confidence, emotional intelligence, teamwork and being articulate. Additionally, I found that in some instances, some high-achieving, academically gifted individuals stated that it felt as though they had an unspoken contractual agreement with their parents. The terms and conditions of the agreement loosely entailed the parents providing the primary needs of shelter and food, with the expectation that their child would bring back good grades and credit to the family name. While it is important that children are given the best chances possible in life, it is more important that they are treated well and feel loved.

With the increasing importance of soft skills, high

academic achievement alone is not enough as it should be balanced with the appropriate soft skills. I have found that people hit a ceiling quite quickly if they lack the necessary soft skills which we explore through this book.

III – Speaking up

Over time, I have observed some academically bright children who have had difficulty finding their voice or being able to cogently express themselves, myself included. This is something I've had to make a conscious effort to improve on each day in almost every interaction with people. Sometimes people find it difficult to believe now that I was once quite shy and inherently introverted. Even with several years of professional working experience and training, I find that I still need to consciously psyche myself up for a particular audience to communicate with impact. The key for parents is that whenever we observe shyness in our children, we should make the effort to give more positive affirmations to encourage and help build their confidence. Additionally, avoiding any scenarios of public humiliation will help preserve our children's confidence while it is developing.

Children who are raised in an environment where they are encouraged to engage and lead conversations with adults appear to have the required soft skills, compared to children raised in an environment where they are not encouraged to 'speak up', and typically only speak when spoken to. It appears that in some communities, it is seen as good manners and respectful if children are quiet and do not speak up. Imagine a set of identical twins separated at birth. One is raised in an environment where 'speak up' is encouraged and nurtured strategically. In effect, being socialised according to the framework discussed in this book, to be: confident, outgoing, articulate, creative and happy. The other twin is raised with no strategy or defined culture that is regularly reinforced. These two children raised within these different environments will inevitably have different life trajectories – with the one nurtured to 'speak up' being more impactful than his or her counterpart because of the difference in their nurturing. This may lead to distinctively different career paths where the more successful candidate will be more likely to demonstrate the sought-after workplace leadership skill set. The cases where children are not intentionally encouraged to be more confident and personable, are lost opportunities for parents to help their children become more outgoing and charismatic. My husband and I observed among our children that some were naturally charismatic and some not so. Therefore, for the ones who were not, through gentle nurturing nudges, we coached them to become more outgoing. For example, we'd explain to one of our daughters that although she is multi-talented and very capable, unless she was more personable and learnt how to demonstrate and articulate her skills through speaking up, most people may never know her true potential and the creative ideas she has. The key is recognising that innate technical abilities can only take you so far and being able to demonstrate what you are capable of is just as important. The reality in which we find ourselves dictates that, in essence, you have to be able to show your skills and abilities. Paradoxically, the most successful people or products aren't necessarily always the best quality – positioning and a good marketing strategy is key in the success of any brand or product.

IV – Praise: the 10-to-1 rule

Children get a self-esteem boost when their efforts are acknowledged and rewarded. Contrastingly, children who are criticised all the time lose confidence and enthusiasm, which in turn affects their school performance, attitude and they sometimes grow up being critical themselves.

I learnt about the 10-to-1 rule from attending a parenting seminar where the keynote speaker advised all parents to aim to give approximately ten praises for every criticism of their child. There are benefits to praise and the key is striking the right balance. From personal experience the praise I received from my family growing up from a young age was empowering, as it meant that I grew up with a sense of self-worth and healthy esteem. Through my teenage years, it meant I was unfazed by praise or compliments from other people, as I was already used to receiving compliments at home. In some ways, this made me a relatively confident and grounded person. An additional benefit of this was that through my teenage years I didn't succumb to peer pressure, and people could not easily pull the wool over my eyes through superficial compliments with ulterior motives. For these reasons, my husband and I ensure that we fortify our children's confidence and self-esteem, reassuring them through praise and regular communication. This is something that I believe is essential, especially in this age of social media explosion, where people are constantly seeking validation and compliments through 'likes' on their posts on Facebook or Instagram.

Let me share an example about the positive impact of praise on an eight-year-old. Let us call her Sophie. One day during the long summer holiday, Sophie decided to help around the house tidying up the kitchen sink area; the mugs, cups, dishes, and cutlery all put away in the right place. The parents stated that they were pleasantly surprised as they had no idea she even knew where everything was kept. Sometimes, as parents, we underestimate how much our children absorb from observing us. Sophie's parents were impressed by her proactivity and sense of responsibility, and praised her copiously. It seemed the more praise Sophie received, the more enthusiastic she became about helping out, beaming with pride and self-satisfaction. For example, as a result of the praise Sophie had received, the parents observed that she felt compelled to do even more. She completed additional tasks, such as folding away the washing, ensuring it was arranged in piles per owner, and she helped to take her younger sibling's clothes to his bedroom. While in the bedroom, she proactively tidied away any loose toys, folding away blankets and anything else that seemed out of place, each time earning more and more praise. She then moved on to tidy her parents' room, folding away clothes left lying around, to the extent that her parents had to eventually ask her to stop and rest. Sophie's parents were amazed at how Sophie just carried on because of the praise she received.

28

The same principle also works for adults; the more we show gratitude and appreciation, the more people want to do for us, going above and beyond to be helpful.

Meghan, the senior executive, explains that she is careful when she praises her children, ensuring that the praise is targeted towards the effort and for participation. For example, she will say to her son, "You have done very well by putting that away." However, she does not just praise for praise's sake. Sometimes she also asks reflective questions to improve her children's self-awareness, such as, "How do you think you did on that task? Did you do that well? How could you have done it better?" Meghan acknowledges that while school results are important, she ensures that she praises her children for their effort, so that even when the results are not great, she still acknowledges the child's effort to encourage and motivate them.

According to Meghan, her son and daughter are wired differently and she shares some insights about how she adapts her approach for both of them. For example, she explains that her son, Andrew, is naturally cautious, therefore she tries to push boundaries in order to encourage him to be more confident and daring. Meghan shares a story from a trip to the local park. She encourages Andrew to climb to the top of the climbing frame as naturally he would not want to. This self-confessed mild 'pushy mum' tries to coach her children to overcome their fears so that the experience of the small victory increases their confidence to try new things. Pushy parenting describes strict or demanding parents who challenge their children to attain high levels of scholastic and academic achievement. Meghan states that she has a nuanced approach to this, ensuring there is some balance between academics and fun interests. She shares how she ensures her children practise and keep practising a particular skill or problem until it becomes easier to solve, and encouraging her children to learn from their failures.

It is important to state at this point that the purpose of this book is not about promoting the concept of pushy parenting, but rather about nurturing your children to maximise their potential through discovering and building on their talents and interests.

Meghan admits that she has outsourced some chores because she works full time. However, she is strategic about what she outsources, and is very selective about her choice of a nanny or childminder. Meghan typically hires students who offer childcare services on a part-time basis. Her rationale is that these student childcarers are academic, and for example, the carer doing their homework alongside the children is encouraging to the children. I suspect that every family situation will be different and different types of childcare providers will be used; there is no one size fits all.

The perils of praise

As much as praise is important, it is critical to get the balance right. In an environment where there is a clear superstar, if one child is being praised all the time, this may lead to resentment from the rest of the siblings. However, if everyone gets their fair share of praise and is acknowledged for the complementary skills they bring to the family or team dynamic, it will lead to a healthier and balanced ecosystem of mutual appreciation and respect.

A key takeaway here is not to reward abilities that come naturally too much, but instead reward the relative effort applied by the child on a particular activity or interest. For example, Meghan states that her son appears to be naturally good at several sports. However, she is careful not to praise too much based on his natural ability, instead ensuring both her son and daughter get similar levels of praise focused on the effort they applied to an activity or challenge.

Therefore, in helping to develop a child's confidence, it is important to respect the differences between each child, understanding what they like and dislike. Rose, the young lady in her mid-twenties, recalls how whenever she was scolded in public the embarrassment was crippling to her confidence. This contrasts with others of a similar age and background who stated that getting scolded in public did not bother them too much, and that they therefore coped and recovered better from what other, more sensitive types would perceive to be a public humiliation. In any case, it will be considered safe to avoid publicly humiliating your child.

V – Be present

Sometimes the best way to demonstrate love is to be present. According to a BBC Radio 4 study, being more present in our children's day-to-day activities could lead to reduced drug problems later on. This study found that children who grow up with a lack of confidence as a result of their parents' absence sometimes end up abusing drugs as a means of escape, to compensate for any feelings of inadequacy.

Through the focus research group, I found that in some cases, 15 years later, some children still feel the upset of not seeing their parents in the crowd at their performance events. Rose explains how this influenced her career choice options as she avoided certain paths that she felt would reduce her presence in her children's lives. She shares some of the stories from within her medical practitioner's circle about certain specialists or consultants who do not get to see their family as much they'd like. She recalls stories from the children of these specialist practitioners who felt they did not have a close relationship with their parents because of their parents' specialisation, as this contributed to their parents' reduced presence at home. Rose states that she wished her parents were more available and attended more of her school performances instead of sending representatives. This is insightful, as it suggests that there are some roles that children do not want covered by a substitute from their 'village'. There are occasions and events to which sending anyone else may not do – children just want their parents to be there, to share that moment with them, especially when they see that their friends have their own parents present. This will, of course, require some balancing as each situation will be different.

Understandably, it can be challenging to juggle work commitments and be present in all of the different activities that our children are interested or involved in. However, it is important to make every effort where possible. I have observed that children get a boost of confidence when they see their parents in the crowd doting on them, cheering them on and getting involved.

Some examples of events that we make an effort to be present at include:

- School events
- Sporting events
- Gymnastics competitions
- Church productions
- Choir productions
- Drama performances

VI – Be involved

It is important for parents to partner with their children's school, ensuring open dialogue with the teachers. Children also feel more confident and are happier when they see their parents involved with school activities. Although it may not always be practical to become school governors, we can find pockets of opportunities to get involved, from fundraising events, sports days to school trips. My children get very excited when we take time off to attend their school or extra-curricular events, especially when they see both parents cheering them on, although in later years they preferred that we behaved cool and not embarrass them from cheering too loud. It's an evolutionary journey.

It is also important to ensure appropriate balance. Children tend to become quite competitive after a confidence boost and want to impress. I am conscious of this when I attend my children's events and I try to ensure there is appropriate balance so my child does not feel under pressure to win in every activity by encouraging them either way.

Notwithstanding, over the years, my children have occasionally asked me why I do not come into the school every week, like the other 'good mums' helping with swimming, sewing and supporting the school in various ways. I believe it is commendable for the parents who are able to support in this way; however, understandably, this is not possible for all parents. The key is to find and take up any opportunities to get involved. During one of the school fundraising Christmas events, I decided to take an afternoon off work to volunteer and run one of the stands. I remember how excited my daughter was when I told her about it. During the event, I observed a sense of pride and belonging each time she walked into the school hall and saw me cheerfully operating my table, trying to sell as many toys and sweets as possible. On other occasions, I have volunteered to go on school trips to help chaperone. On one particular occasion, I was delighted to initially have the opportunity as a helper on a school trip; although it turned out to be a challenging experience, it was also fulfilling. Additionally, it gave me some insight and perspective about how hard the teachers work, and therefore a deeper appreciation for their efforts. Open dialogue and consistent communication is essential. On the occasions where it is not possible to attend events, I have found that it helps to take the time to explain and discuss the reasons with my children, showing great interest in the event and following up afterwards.

VII – Prepare to stay ahead

Children are more confident in school when they turn up prepared. Parents can boost their children's confidence by helping them stay on top of their schoolwork, and by being engaged with the school.

Staying on track with the daily learning and development objectives is an important way to build your child's confidence. This can be achieved by:

- keeping up with your child's regular reading schedule,
- helping them broaden their vocabulary through practising their words list, and
- nurturing their maths skills from early on.

Early numeracy skills have always been a good indicator of academic, as well as financial, success. A study based on analysis of existing data from more than 35,000 preschoolers across the US, Canada and England by the US National Library of Medicine of the National Institutes of Health, published in the *Journal of Developmental Psychology*, has shown that:

> "Early math skills have the greatest predictive power, followed by reading and then attention skills."

In recent times, there have been more initiatives and campaigns to develop children's financial literacy. Drawing on my maths background and over 15 years of working within the financial services industry at the time of writing,

I have developed a framework and some exercises to help parents fill this gap. This is covered in more detail in Chapter 7, with an example scenario that can be used to help your child become more financially informed. Children can get involved at an early age at the basic level of simply totalling up the items in a shopping basket, and by practising their mental maths skills. Maths is one of those subjects that some parents either enjoy or loathe. For the latter, perhaps get a maths tutor to assist in the development of this critical skill in your child if necessary. You can find details of free apps that can be downloaded to support your child in the additional resources section at the end of this book.

According to a 2007 study by co-author and Northwestern University researcher Greg Duncan:

> "Controlling for IQ, family income, gender, temperament, type of previous educational experience, and whether children came from single or two parent families, the study found that the mastery of early math concepts on school entry was the very strongest predictor of future academic success."

Preparing ahead

There are numerous ways that parents can support their children to prepare for events, and not necessarily just on the academic front.

Rose, from the focus group, shares a story about how her father helped her to prepare for her first interview, coaching her about the importance of making the right first impression.

I suspect that some children may have their first interview experience around the age of ten as part of their secondary school application process. However, I share this story as it is relevant and provides useful insight. Rose explains how she found this initial interview experience quite draining, trying to present her best self for the duration of it. However, what encouraged her were the words of her father, motivating her through the preparation process; he reassured her that even if it felt draining at a point, she should just persevere, as she will have all the time to recover afterwards. The incentive that she would leave the interviewer with the best possible impression of her was encouraging. Although this was not an easy experience, nonetheless she felt reassured by her parent's words and involvement, reminding her that with practice it would become more comfortable. After the event, the comments and encouragement that Rose received from her father were equally important. She recalls her father managing her expectations in the event of an unsuccessful outcome. She appreciated her father telling her not to be discouraged if she did not get the desired result the first time round, and should instead see this as part of the preparation for the top prize to come eventually. A consistent theme through the focus group was that the young adults, now well into their twenties, had fond memories of these sorts of pep talks and rehearsal sessions with their parents, which they found reassuring.

The school holidays could also be a good opportunity to catch up or prepare for the term ahead, as well as resting and engaging in other fun and extra-curricular activities. During one of the long school holidays, I introduced my children to doing word searches and crossword puzzles to keep them occupied.

We initially completed a few together as a family fun activity, and then individually as a light competition to see who could find the most words. My children became very interested in this, so much so that I also downloaded an app on my phone which helped to keep them occupied during long car journeys or just in general as a pastime. This activity unexpectedly came in handy when my daughter returned to school after the summer holiday. On her first day back in school in Year Four, one of the tasks they completed was to find their classmates' names on a word search. My daughter finished promptly and was able to help some of the other children. This was only possible because she had had a lot of practice over the holiday, learning and mastering the techniques. Although this is not a big deal, it did, however, create an instant impression with her new teacher when she was chosen as the monitor, which as a result boosted her confidence.

Meghan, the senior executive, shares some of the structure and discipline she instils with her children over the summer holidays. For example, she shares the concept of building screen time from study time. Her children's screen time depended on how much time was spent on schoolwork or chores around the house. Meghan shares that this approach has been effective; it has encouraged her children to do more work in order to earn more screen time.

VIII – Grit and building resilience

Through sports, drama or theatre performances, children develop the confidence to perform in front of an audience.

Additionally, developing resilience can contribute to your child's confidence from the self-belief that they can achieve a goal if they put their mind to it. This could go a long way in encouraging them even when they have nobody cheering them on. This is a trait I have observed in one of my children who enjoys various sports activities. I have found that sports activities are a good way to help children develop resilience and perseverance.

> "It is about teaching kids to imagine and commit to a future they want to create."
>
> Angela Duckworth

Psychologist Angela Duckworth won a MacArthur 'genius' grant for her work on this success-driving personality trait called *'grit'*. Grit, which is synonymous with resilience, can be defined as a *'tendency to sustain interest in and effort towards very long-term goals'.* Therefore, 'grit' is an incremental predictive success measure over and beyond IQ, suggesting that:

> "The achievement of difficult goals entails not only talent but also the sustained and focused application of effort over time."

SUMMARY: HOW TO RAISE A MORE CONFIDENT CHILD

1. Allocate early responsibilities such as:

   - making beds
   - tidying up their room
   - sorting laundry
   - setting the washing machine

2. Identify and develop expertise around a core talent

3. Encourage your child to speak up

4. Praise your children, as this leads to:

   - a self-esteem boost
   - increased positivity

But be aware of the perils of praise.

5. Be present:

Children get a boost of confidence when they see their parents in the crowd doting on them, cheering them on and getting involved in their events.

Examples of events include:

- School events
- Sporting events
- Gymnastics competitions
- Church productions
- Choir productions
- Drama performances

6. Be involved:

   - by engaging with and through open dialogue with teachers
   - with school activities, summer fayres or other fundraising events

7. Prepare to stay ahead by:

   - keeping up with the daily learning and development objectives
   - staying on track with your child's regular reading schedule
   - practising words lists
   - teaching maths early on
   - using the holidays to catch up or get ahead
   - helping with interview preparation, i.e. for secondary school

8. Develop grit and build resilience through:

   - playing sports
   - drama performances

Children develop confidence through stepping out of their comfort zone and learning from repetition, from drama productions or sporting events.

CHAPTER 3

Outgoing

"Leadership is about making others better as a result of your presence and making sure that impact lasts in your absence."

Sheryl Sandberg

In Malcolm Gladwell's bestseller *Outliers,* he discusses a particular skill called 'practical intelligence' that allows one to talk their way out of a situation, such as convincing a professor to move you from the morning to the afternoon session. This term, originally coined by psychologist Robert Sternberg, includes things like *'knowing what to say to whom, knowing when to say it, and knowing how to say it for maximum effect'.* Essentially, this knowledge enables people to read situations and get what they want. Although IQ, which measures analytical ability, is innate, social or practical intelligence can be learnt. Interestingly, we learn these skills and attitudes from our families. Social skills and the ability to make friends easily contribute to a better performance. Parents can help children become more outgoing by communicating with them regularly. In *Outliers,* we read about the findings by sociologist Annette Lareau. There are two parenting 'philosophies' and they appear to divide along class lines. One style, referred to as 'concerted cultivation', is where parents actively nurture a child's talents, opinions and skills. Contrastingly, the other style, referred to as 'accomplishment of natural growth', is where parents see the responsibility to care for their children but let them grow and develop on their own. Although one style is not necessarily morally better than the other, in practical terms, concerted cultivation appears to have enormous advantages. According to Lareau, with concerted cultivation, parents are more involved in their children's free time, talking things through with them, reasoning with them, expecting them to question adults, even those in positions of authority. The children learn teamwork, how to cope in structured settings, how to interact comfortably with adults and make special requests. Contrastingly, authority intimidates those nurtured through the style of accomplishment of natural growth, reacting passively, staying in the background and characterised by a sense of distance. From Lareau's study, we learn about Alex, a nine-year-old boy with professional parents. One day on the way to their doctor's appointment, his mother encourages him to think of questions to ask the doctor, and not to be shy. In essence, she is nurturing him to learn to speak up. As a result, Alex makes an impression on the doctor through remembering to raise his questions prepared in advance, thus shifting the balance of power. The point here is to note that this skill of confidently interacting with authority figures isn't inherited but it's as a result of conscious nurturing, teaching the rules of the game of succeeding in our present world.

An article by the National Literacy Trust in 2012, titled *'Family mealtime chat'*, found that:

"A quarter of children do not chat to their family over dinner, leaving them too shy to talk to teachers confidently."

Talking at the table over dinner helps children to become more outgoing and do well at school. Children who talk to their parents during mealtimes are more confident communicators than those who do not, and perform better in general. Set out below are some examples of how to help your child become more outgoing and charismatic:

I – Regular communication

Communicating regularly can help your child to better deal with their feelings and increases your awareness as a parent of behavioural changes. Let me share an example to illustrate this point. Meghan, the senior executive, states that communication is very important and along with her husband, they always talk to their children about their plans and expectations. She states how important it is to set expectations early on so that the children know what they can or cannot do. For example, her children play several team sports, such as cricket – Meghan says that this creates the opportunity to develop skills, such as communication and teamwork. She explains that there is a lot of communication that goes on in a game of cricket. This in turn also helps to build confidence.

Managing expectations

Managing expectations can be reassuring in establishing consistency and building confidence, and not just for children. Let me provide a hypothetical example for illustration. Imagine being on a train that suddenly stops in the middle of a tunnel without any explanation from the driver. Even a two-minute wait not knowing what is going on can be very distressing. Contrast this to the driver communicating and keeping you updated, about why the train has stopped and how long it is likely to be for. Even if advised that the train will be held for 15 minutes, that will be more bearable and acceptable compared to not being given any explanation, and not knowing what is going on even for a short time.

Seize the opportunity

Parents sometimes wrongly assume that because their child is very academic they will automatically flourish and, therefore, they do not feel the need to nurture these softer skills such as confidence, effective communication and resilience, which will enhance their child's potential and the magnitude of their success. For example, taking part in sports can help to develop teamwork and people skills.

One morning I noticed that my daughter looked rather pensive, so I asked her if everything was OK. Although she said everything was fine, I felt that there was something wrong so I persisted. Eventually she mentioned that there was an upcoming athletics trial and she was keen on making the team this year after missing out last year. As she spoke, looking quite upset with her eyes starting to well up, I realised how much this meant to her. I hadn't realised how disappointed she was about not making the team the year before; we just brushed it off at the time and said she could try again next year.

From this encounter, I realised that when it comes to children, the more communication the better and we should take up any opportunity, no matter how fleeting, to find out what is going on in our children's world or troubling their minds. This chance discussion gave me the opportunity to come up with a plan of how to help improve her performance this time. After she shared with me the sort of activities covered during the trials and the ones she needed the most help with, we purchased some of the equipment and dedicated some time to practise at home. This eventually became a team effort – her father took her jogging on a couple of occasions to help with the long-distance running, and I ordered some of the sports items so she could practise some of the throwing exercises in the garden. On the day of the trials, I offered to make her a special breakfast so that she would have the required energy for the trial. In the end, this improved her ability and confidence and she performed better than the previous year. Despite this, she was still not selected for the first team. However, being part of the team as a reserve was a win for her, as she got to wear the team kit. In reality she was still somewhat disappointed but not as much as she would have been had she not made the team at all. This is a good example of how seizing the opportunity to talk gave me, the parent, the opportunity to intervene relatively early and make some positive difference. The following year and thereafter, not only did she make it onto the first team, she became a critical team member, significantly contributing to the school's sporting success.

The key takeaway here is to talk to our children as often as possible and be discerning when we do, as the insight into the issues bothering them is an easy gateway to help boost their performance and happiness. Talking gives the child a chance to voice their thoughts and feelings. The parent gains further insight into their child's strengths and weaknesses so that they know where to support, and the parent and child develop a stronger bond. This can be a challenge in these days of technological advancement and social media explosion; according to research by Ofcom published in 2018, one third of children spend more time online, on smartphones or watching TV, than communicating with their family. This is a lost opportunity; as covered in the previous section, children who do not have mealtimes with their parents, or those who eat in silence, generally avoid speaking up in the classroom or in front of an audience. The knock-on impact is that they are unlikely to put up their hands in class or work as effectively within a team. The consequence of such behaviour is that children could be marked down under the revised national curriculum, which focuses heavily on speaking and listening skills according to the National Literacy Trust.

The overwhelming conclusion indicates that conversations at home between parents and children are critical to their performance and all-round well-being.

Scheduled one-to-ones

In most corporate organisations, one-to-ones are scheduled regularly between managers and staff to ensure a regular touch point. These catch-ups are useful for career progression and for tracking deliverables.

Leveraging this practice, we started to schedule regular one-to-one meetings with our children to discuss their week: anything bothering them, what we as their parents could have done better, anything we said or did that upset them during the week and so on. Sometimes as we rush through the week managing all our commitments and pressing responsibilities, with some days going better than others, this gives us the opportunity to slow down, take the time to reflect and clarify any miscommunication for better understanding. My husband and I typically take it in turns and we have found that these regular meetings give us useful insights, as well as the opportunity to iron out any concerns or resentful feelings building up.

These meetings have also helped to resolve sibling rivalry. This process was initiated when we noticed that the children started bickering more than normal and we decided to have separate discussions with each of them to understand what the underlying issues were. To incentivise the initial discussions, we suggested that we set apart some time to have a snack or juice with Mummy or Daddy to talk about anything on their minds, in confidence. Following the initial meeting, they started to look forward to their one-on-one meetings, choosing either parent depending on what they wanted to discuss, sometimes making a list through the week of the agenda points they wanted to cover, taking more initiative and enforcing their meeting slots if they were missed.

My husband and I often discuss how these regular meetings have helped us to improve our approach and the increased self-awareness of some of the things that we do or say inadvertently that affects their self-esteem. This process has helped us to manage the dynamics between the children better, and other benefits include:

- Developing trust to confide in the parents
- Encouraging open communication
- Empowering the children to speak up and believe that their views and opinions matter
- Strengthening the bond through the trust created between parent and child and between the children

II – Developing a sense of humour

Children are creatures of habit, especially in their early years. Children nurtured in an environment where they see their parents laughing and sharing jokes are more likely to eventually emulate what they see and, through the process, understand the importance of not taking themselves too seriously. Having a sense of humour is a key attribute of being charismatic.

The findings from the focus group indicated that in some cases children lacked this opportunity to be personable with their parents. Some had a serious relationship with their parents and only appeared to discuss serious or transactional matters. Although this is not necessarily bad, it is important to get the balance right. This suggests that children with a simple relationship with their parents share humour and do not take themselves too seriously.

Meghan, the senior executive, states that from when her son was five years old, she taught him to be able to laugh at himself and look at things objectively, seeing the funny side through having the strength of character to not be too sensitive or easily offended.

Another candidate from the focus group, Mark, introduced earlier, explains that, as a middle child, he felt he needed to be exceptional, otherwise no one would remember him. In his case, Mark says that as a third-born and second son, he sometimes felt that he needed to differentiate himself and be more charismatic in order to be memorable. Mark also acknowledges that this was potentially a pivotal position because some children may not care about finding their unique talents to help them stand out in the family, whereas others might do, to the extent that it affects their confidence. However, in Mark's case, charisma was his standout factor, which was partly developed from being involved in a variety of extra-curricular activities and social events while in boarding school.

Birth order impact

In the 1930s, the Austrian psychotherapist Alfred Adler was the first to study birth order and its effect on personality. Since then, there have been numerous studies, sometimes contradictory, about how a child's birth order – whether the eldest, in the middle or the youngest – affects their personality. Some stereotypes – that older children are more responsible, middle children trying to find their place and the youngest acts the baby – are not new, and not necessarily true in all instances. However, first-borns are more likely to have the experience of being in charge of younger siblings, and therefore better positioned to develop leadership skills early on. First-borns also tend to be more pressured at school as parents may push their own expectations and dreams onto them.

However, according to Dr Catherine Salmon, author of *The Secret Power of Middle Children*, contrary to popular belief, middle children are often highly successful entrepreneurs. They develop good psychological skills from watching how the eldest interacts with parents. The last-born, also referred to as the baby of the family, is often seen by psychologists as a charmer who takes risks. Again, these are just generalisations and may not necessarily apply in every family dynamic.

According to Frank Sulloway, a birth order expert, last-born children score well in personality tests on 'agreeableness' or getting along with others.

When it comes to career options, a study by Disney suggested that birth order has a 'tangible and marked effect' on your child's career. The research found that the eldest child is more ambitious. However, the same research found that middle children are most likely to be CEOs, Olympians and authors. It appears that this 'middle child syndrome' has its positives, as middle children are 30% more likely than their siblings to be a company CEO. Research from parenting expert Michael Grose has also found that only children are more confident, articulate and likely to use their imagination than other children with siblings.

While these are all interesting research studies on birth order, they are only generalisations. Children are unique with their own innate capabilities and aspirations. While these studies make for good discussions and debates, I would not rely heavily on them, and they have been provided here for awareness.

Most people like a good laugh and, therefore, may naturally enjoy the company of someone who makes them laugh. Some of the best speakers I have listened to typically try to infuse some humour into speeches and talks in order to keep the audience engaged. My husband and I share jokes with our children regularly, and they look forward to sharing any new jokes they learn with us. An additional benefit of these jokes is that they can sometimes be witty and it gives the children an opportunity to demonstrate some wit and a sense of humour.

There are several resources online or in bookshops that families can access to encourage laughter together.

III – Teach social skills and self-awareness

Helping your child develop social skills through emotional intelligence is one of the most important things you can do to prepare them for a brighter future. Researchers from Pennsylvania State University and Duke University tracked more than 700 children from across the US, between kindergarten and age 25. They found a strong link between children's social skills in nursery and their success as adults 20 years later. The study showed that socially competent children who could cooperate with other children easily, understand their feelings and resolve problems independently, were more likely to lead a contented adult life compared to those with little social skills. According to the study:

> "From an early age, these skills can determine whether a child goes to college or prison, and whether they end up employed or addicted."

Therefore, helping children learn how to manage conflict is important, even just the reassurance that it is normal to fall out with friends sometimes. For example, helping them to manage any negative emotion they might be feeling about a disagreement can by achieved by rationalising their feelings. Reflecting on the circumstances that led up to the incident, what went wrong and how to improve the outcome the next time, can be empowering, leading to better relationship management.

IV – Teach morals, kindness and integrity

Good morals, kindness and integrity are timeless and important qualities. As parents, we have a pastoral responsibility to help our children develop these qualities. The easiest approach that some families have adopted and practise is through religious or spiritual studies, assigning key memory verses or quotations that reinforce diligence, kindness, wisdom and integrity. I believe in not withholding kindness; it should always be given away – you can give it away but gain from that yourself.

However, depending on your religious beliefs and philosophies, you may choose to substitute this with your chosen philosophy as part of your value system. This is further discussed in Chapter 9: Mind-set and Values.

SUMMARY: HOW TO NURTURE A MORE CHARISMATIC CHILD

1. Have regular communication by:

   - managing expectations
   - engaging in conversations over dinner
   - having scheduled one-on-one time
   - limiting time spent online, watching TV and on other devices

2. Share appropriate jokes on a regular basis to help develop a sense of humour.

3. Teach social skills and self-awareness.

4. Teach morals, kindness and integrity.

CHAPTER 4

Articulate

"Leadership is a way of thinking, a way of acting and, most importantly, a way of communicating."

Simon Sinek

Studies have shown over and over that the number of words spoken to a child in the first three years of their life, has a strong correlation with their performance and literacy skills as they get older. The way the parents speak to their child is also significant. The impact on the child's brain who has engaged in a lot of 'chat' with their parents will have an exponential cognitive advantage – over income, ethnicity or parents' education level – and do better in all academic subjects.

According to Mrs Wordsmith, an innovative vocabulary programme:

> "A rich vocabulary is the passport to academic success in every subject, therefore early development of broad vocabulary is important."

A 2012 article published in the *Financial Times* found that 'the first three years of life are key to shaping the brain and much of a child's destiny'. According to the research by Sally Grantham-McGregor, emerita professor of international child health at University College London, children stimulated in infancy had higher IQs, better mental health, experienced lower rates of criminal behaviour and earnt higher wages than their unstimulated peers. This was based on the 1980s research by community health workers in Jamaica who found that coaching mothers to play and chat with their children, as well as ensuring good nutrition, significantly shaped much of the child's destiny. Essentially, a young child's nutrition, sleep, relationships and nurturing experiences shape his or her brain. Unfortunately, so do bad experiences.

> "The first five years of life are critical for the development of language and cognitive skills. By kindergarten entry, steep social gradients in reading and math ability, with successively poorer outcomes for children in families of lower social class, are already apparent. Early cognitive ability is, in turn, predictive of later school performance, educational attainment, and health in adulthood. Early life represents a time period of most equality and yet, beginning with in utero conditions and extending through early childhood, a wide range of socially stratified risk and protective factors may begin to place children on different trajectories of cognitive development."

Neal Halfon, Director, UCLA Center for Healthier Children, Families and Communities

The magic number: three

In most cases a child's fate is sealed before age three, according to an article by Simon Kuper published in the *Financial Times*. The gap in development at age three between the child of university-educated parents who knows 1,200 words on average, and those from disadvantaged backgrounds who know about 400 words rarely closes after that. According to research by the Harvard University's Center on the Developing Child, this clearly suggests that societies should prioritise these early years, to boost future health, productivity and equality, while also reducing crime. However, the reality is that parents are responsible for infancy, which is fine for children with responsible parents who know or seek out what to do. But what happens to the fate and potential of children whose parents, even with the best intentions, are perhaps unaware or fail to invest the time and resources on these early years which yield more significant developmental benefits than any other phase of life? Although, to put things in perspective, on average some turn out just fine, or even exceed expectations, as demonstrated by the story of Michael Fuller in Chapter 9.

Some practical ways of helping children become more articulate are as follows:

I – Broader vocabulary

The mastery of words is a key skill, as the ability to articulate and negotiate skilfully can be very effective. Therefore, equipping children with this useful skill gives them a competitive edge in a world where great and respected leaders exhibit strong oratory competence. The expansion of vocabulary and the ability to express yourself in a way that makes you compelling, impactful and inspirational is critical because:

- knowledge is transferred through words
- language is the mastery of communication
- authority and power can be limited with weak use of words; it doesn't matter how great an idea is if it's not delivered convincingly
- generals inspire troops with words
- presidents, prime ministers and leaders win and inspire people with words delivered effectively.

Therefore, a key skill for a leader or aspiring influencer is the effective use of language. I have learnt over the years that the more words a child knows, the higher their reading age classification and the better their results. It is that simple. Communication is an art and a critical skill to master through life, as there is always an area of communication to improve on, depending on the audience. I still consciously work on improving almost on a daily basis despite my years of professional training in this area. Over the last 16 years, I have worked in leading global institutions with rigorous graduate training programmes and attended some of the best educational institutions in the world. I state this because effective communication in any and every circumstance is crucial and improvement is an ongoing learning process.

II – Daily reading

There are countless research studies which strongly indicate a marked difference in performance between children who read regularly and those who do not. We know that children can easily adopt habits. Therefore, once reading becomes part of the expected daily routine, it becomes easier to manage as your child will require infrequent reminders. Additionally, from personal experience, children look forward to incentives such as end-of-term awards and recognition for reading consistently. This feel-good factor is likely to lead to a more confident and happier child.

To further illustrate how parents can help their children, let me share a story from Mark, the Oxford University PhD scholar from the focus group. Mark shares that his parents encouraged him and his siblings to read a lot early on. He remembers reading big novels from an early age which helped him to become more articulate with a broad range of vocabulary. Mark recalls having a set reading time, such that when other children and neighbours knocked on the door unexpectedly inviting him and his siblings to play, they would politely decline to reinforce the rule to their friends about their reading time.

Library visits

Mark states that going to the library on a weekly basis to select books made an early impression on him. He also had responsibility for remembering when the books were due to be returned. As we discussed earlier in Chapter 2, confidence can be developed through having responsibilities.

In this case, membership of the local library came with responsibilities. Although Mark admits it was not always fun and was actually seen as a chore initially, eventually he became more enthusiastic about reading and looked forward to going to the library to change his books. Regular library visits became the norm in his family, being built into their weekly routine. Mark, who was predominantly raised in a single-parent home and only saw his father occasionally, remembers that his father would always have a new book for him whenever they met. This further honed his love of reading and broadened his vocabulary over time.

Meghan, the executive in financial services, provides an alternative perspective on her and her husband's preferred approach in broadening their children's vocabulary. She states that they have always spoken to their children using the same vocabulary as they would to an adult. Meghan states that they never assumed that the child would not understand. Instead, they would use other synonymous terms until their son or daughter understood, broadening their vocabulary in the process. Meghan shares that through articulating things in two or three different ways that mean the same thing, they found that they seldom needed to simplify their language when talking to their children.

Some of the different ways I have used to broaden my children's vocabulary include:

- playing games such as Scrabble, Articulate and charades
- completing word searches
- encouraging role-playing and open communication at home

- leading/chairing family discussions such as Bible study, ensuring everyone is engaged and participating in the discussions. This also encourages applying emotional intelligence to pull people into discussions and encouraging them to speak up and share their views and opinions to add to the discussions.

SUMMARY: HOW TO NURTURE A MORE ARTICULATE CHILD

1. Broaden vocabulary from daily reading
2. Nurture a love of reading
3. Practise leading and chairing discussions at home
4. Taking part in debates

CHAPTER 5

Creative

"Innovation distinguishes between a leader and a follower."

Steve Jobs

There is a link between creativity and critical thinking, and interestingly, critical thinking is not currently part of the national school curriculum. However, an easy and practical way to help children develop this essential skill is through empowering them to challenge things and ask questions.

Creativity and innovation are critical to success in any industry and profession. Creativity can be improved and fostered in anyone's life, which is why it is a key skill to learn from a young age. For example, encouraging children to ask 'why' will result in them learning to judge what 'fake news' is so that they do not become naïve or vulnerable. Some of the benefits of developing critical thinking skills are:

- better communication skills

- empowering children to feel that they can make a positive difference through better understanding
- improved playground behaviour
- more resilience
- improved team-working skills

Critical thinking

While literacy and numeracy are equally important skills for children to develop, critical thinking, also referred to as 'reasoning skills', which some children get exposed to through the secondary school entrance exams for selective schools, enhances children's knowledge and understanding. There are numerous ways we can help children develop this useful skill. Set out below are some of the ways by which children can develop critical thinking:

- by exploring and analysing their own views in different situations
- through independent thinking and sharing their views and opinions.

According to Lisa Phillips, author of *The Artistic Edge: 7 Skills Children Need to Succeed in an Increasingly Right Brain World* (see Figure 3), creativity and critical thinking skills, which improve confidence, can be developed through the arts.

Nowadays, it would appear that children are being exposed to social media too early. Research published by *Internet Matters* suggests that developing critical thinking skills in children can be a preventative strategy for vulnerable children.

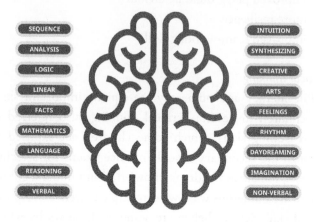

Figure 3: The Different Sides of the Brain

For example, I expose my children to some news headlines tailored to be age appropriate, but I also ensure that there is some balance, so that the exposure does not create anxiety issues, by being available to answer any questions and provide clarification where necessary. My husband and I are selective about the type of news to expose our children to when we can control it.

From the focus group, Mark describes himself as not particularly creative, although he is comfortable with taking risks and is not afraid of failure. Mark opens up about his childhood desire to be a footballer, but his parents did not consider it a reliable career option as opportunities to 'make it' were few and far between. As a result, Mark felt he grew up with little creativity, including limited exposure to developing any musical talent, as his parents didn't nurture these attributes either. This is an example of how parents inadvertently stifle their children's creativity in favour of academic excellence, resulting in lost potential. In Mark's case, although he has ended up as a very successful management consultant working for the world's leading management consultancy, he still feels that had he been more creative, it would have been advantageous.

Rose from the focus group, who is now a medical doctor, shares the story of how she was scouted for a football team when she was in primary school, but her parents were not interested in her pursuing a sports career and saw it as a distraction rather than an opportunity at the time. Although Rose is a very successful medical doctor today, she still sees this as a lost opportunity. She states that she enjoys football and believes she may have been playing professionally today. However, she is not too disappointed with her current outcome as she enjoys being a doctor and helping people.

The key point is really the opportunity cost of limiting our children's interests. I believe we should expose children to as many varied interests as possible. For example, helping children to develop their musical talent is very important on several fronts, because being able to play a musical instrument is not the only benefit. There is the added benefit of using a different part of the brain that would otherwise be inactive. The impact of using more parts of the brain and the associated benefits can be exponential. Similarly, learning other languages encourages the use of more parts of the brain that would otherwise be dormant. This is why it is critical that children are exposed to as many interests as possible when their brains are most receptive. Limited exposure means there is a risk of not discovering all of their potential and the erroneous conclusion of thinking they are not good at very much. For example, if you never buy a sketchpad and attempt to draw, how can you be sure you cannot draw? Therefore, the earlier children are exposed, the more creative they are likely to be. This also gives them the opportunity for developing mastery, which is achieved over time as described by the 10,000 hours rule. This theory suggests that practising any skill for 10,000 hours is sufficient to make you an expert. This common rule of thumb was popularised by Malcolm Gladwell in his bestseller *Outliers: The Story of Success*.

Set out below are the benefits of exposing children to the arts and other creative outlets.

1 – Problem solving

Being able to think on their feet, approaching tasks from different perspectives, and thinking 'outside of the box' may distinguish your child. For example, according to Lisa Phillips, author of *The Creative Edge*, by reciting a monologue in different ways, or composing new rhythms, children will have more opportunities to practise thinking creatively, and the more it will become second nature as they get older.

Meghan, the senior executive, shares that her son is naturally creative. Therefore, nurturing this skill was easy

– through imaginative play, thinking about solutions to problems and learning to solve his own problems. She explains that she typically asks questions about problems and listens to how her son processes the problem in his attempt to try to solve it. Innovative thinking and creativity can be developed through problem solving. For example, through role-playing, children develop problem-solving skills without even realising it. Fine-tuning this skill over time will lead to increased creativity as they get older.

Essentially, being creative and innovative is the essence of wanting to do things better. One morning at the end of a very busy week, with a few things still unchecked on the to-do list, I woke up earlier than usual to go downstairs and catch up on the week, and get a head start on the day before everyone else woke up. My plan was to respond to the various permission slips for school trips and half-term parties/playdate invitations. I dedicated 30 minutes to the laundry and then another 45 minutes or so reading over materials for a meeting later that day. However, from around 6:45 a.m. I became sidetracked with my two-year-old son's newfound obsession with Henry the vacuum cleaner. It was a strange infatuation where he could not seem to stay away from it, but at the same time, he seemed to run away when it is switched on. It was interesting to observe that he could keep himself entertained with Henry for up to 30 minutes. Whenever I glanced over at him, he looked preoccupied with taking the hose apart and then connecting it back again. He would tentatively attempt to switch it on but also back-step simultaneously. I could not help but be amused. If only I had known that all the times before when I made futile efforts to keep him entertained, especially when he wanted to go out to play in the garden at 6 a.m., all I needed to have done was to bring out the vacuum cleaner. As I became more intrigued about his obsession, I decided to do some research into why a toddler would be so fond of Henry the vacuum cleaner.

This curiosity exposed me to one of the simplest yet successful innovations that had been right under my nose all this time. A smile, literally. According to a marketing blog by Lee Gilbert:

> "Henry came into the world in the Beaminster, Dorset factory in the UK in 1981. Ever since he was first introduced into the vacuum market, Henry has brought domestic joy to the lives of over a million people – a superlative achievement and a popularity that hasn't declined."

That morning I learnt first-hand the fundamentals of innovation. Sometimes the key to 'doing something better' is to do it with a smile, or in other words, with a positive attitude. It seems no matter how much work Henry has to do, he always does it with a smile. Perhaps this is the solution for all grunt work, and maybe the next big domestic innovation will be to put a smiley face on the iron. The point of sharing this story is that we can all be innovative if we find ways to either solve a problem or do something better, and sometimes all we need is a positive approach and the desire to put a smile on someone's face.

II – Perseverance and dedication

Children can develop perseverance from learning musical instruments through continuous practice. Efforts that result in a finished product or performance contribute to healthier habits such as valuing others' contributions and commitment to the success of the finished product, which in turn boosts confidence and creativity.

III – Focus

Staying focused takes discipline; maintaining the balance between listening and contributing involves good concentration and focus. According to Phillips, in an ensemble, participants are typically required to think about how their role contributes to the big picture. This is beneficial for developing a more rounded perspective from an early age, and children who develop this skill also see improvements in their confidence and creativity.

IV – Emotional intelligence

According to research by *The Hearing Journal*, 70% of communication is non-verbal. Through stage and drama performances, children learn to communicate different emotions through body language. Additionally, this leads to increased creativity and situational awareness, by being able to understand body language from an early age.

V – Responding appropriately to feedback

Feedback is essential for developing self-awareness and is key to ongoing personal development. Through receiving regular feedback, either in sports or some other extra-curricular activities, children come to understand that this is part of learning. This way they do not become defensive or upset when they receive strong feedback. Over time, the expectation is that feedback will be received as a helpful gift for self-improvement and improved creativity, such that by the time children get to their teens they will have learnt how to receive and apply feedback positively.

VI – Teamwork and accountability

Teamwork works! Participation in performances that require collaboration and team effort, such as a Christmas panto production, provides an opportunity for children to work together, sharing responsibility and accommodating others to accomplish a positive team goal. For example, when a child has a part to play in a drama or dance production, they realise that their contribution is necessary for the success of the whole piece. This in turn leads to increased confidence in the value of their role, no matter how small. When children get the opportunity to work in teams, whether in school or collaborating with their siblings at home for a role-play, they get used to the idea that their actions and role affect other people. The combined impact of the individual contributions results in higher team performance, because the whole is more than the sum of the parts.

SUMMARY: DEVELOPING CREATIVE SKILLS

How to become more creative:

1. Practise creativity by approaching tasks from different perspectives

2. Innovative thinking and creativity can be achieved through problem solving and asking questions

3. Children can develop creativity through learning musical instruments, or participating in sports or drama productions

4. Through drama, children can learn to communicate and read body language, which leads to improved emotional intelligence as well as it being a creative outlet

5. Through collaboration with either siblings at home or friends in school for a role-play, for sports events or productions, children get used to the idea that their actions and role affect other people and the final output. This process of working in teams and sharing ideas can lead to increased creativity in general

Benefits of creativity:

I   – Problem solving
II   – Perseverance and dedication
III – Focus
IV   – Emotional intelligence
V   – Responding appropriately to feedback
VI   – Teamwork and accountability

CHAPTER 6

Happy

"When I was five years old, my mother always told me that happiness was the key to life. When I went to school they asked me what I wanted to be when I grew up. I wrote down 'happy'. They told me I didn't understand the assignment, and I told them they didn't understand life."

John Lennon

A child development study in 2014 by the University of Minnesota found that children who received 'sensitive caregiving', where parents respond to their child's signals promptly in their early years, did better in academic tests in childhood. This group of children also had healthier relationships and greater academic attainment in their thirties.

A lifelong study led by University College London (UCL), published in *The Independent* newspaper, that has tracked over 5,000 people from their birth in 1946 in England,

Scotland and Wales, has found that children of parents who are warmer and less psychologically controlling grow up happier. According to *Psychology Today,* psychological control is the extent to which parents try to control the child's emotional state or beliefs. For example, they may use guilt induction or make the child feel that they have been disrespectful if they do not do what their parents want. Children raised by psychologically controlling parents tend to exhibit signs of low self-esteem. The same study found:

"Examples of psychologically controlling behaviour, included invasions of children's privacy, an unwillingness to let children make their own decisions, and fostering dependence. Parents are vitally important to the mental well-being of future generations."

Dr Mai Stafford, Medical Research Council, UCL

Although there are some sensitive topics covered in this section of the book, this is not to point any fingers but to create awareness. I like to believe we all try our best within our means as parents to give our children the best we can. Therefore, while out of scope for the purpose of this book, policies that reduce financial pressures on parents could contribute to better nurturing, and therefore better outcomes for society. It is no surprise that the role of a parent is very important in nurturing their children's happiness well into adulthood. According to the authors of this lifelong study:

"The impact of parenting on a child's mental well-being lasts from adolescence right through to their sixties."

The same study monitored the mental health of participants between the ages of 13 and 64, and found that reduced economic pressures on parents and healthier work–life balance could contribute to better relationships with their children. Most parents naturally desire to be their best and want to raise happy and well-rounded children that will eventually contribute positively to society, but unfortunately socio-economic pressures can make it a challenge or impossible to achieve.

Happy memories

It is interesting to learn which memories people treasure from their childhood. Sometimes the most insignificant of events can have a lasting impact. For example, Rose has fond memories of her father taking her and her brothers to the local park to play football at the weekends. She states that she placed a lot of value on having her parents present during her early years.

However, Mark recalls the few occasions he remembers the family spending time together discussing some Bible stories and praying together. Although he didn't appreciate it at the time, he now thinks of those sessions as special because they were some of the few times he remembers the family spending time together. Other than that, Mark says he has no memories of his father spending much personal

Picture 1: Work-life balance

time with him. As a result, he channelled those feelings of abandonment into becoming more resilient. Despite this, he still wishes his parents had been more available and listened more. He states he would have been more confident if he'd felt that he had a voice that was listened to at home. As an eternal optimist, Mark highlights the positives of the situation, as he states that these circumstances contributed to him being low maintenance and easy to please. However, Mark believes that it is still good to be heard, and having a voice at home makes it easier to speak up outside.

Set out below are some of the best practices summarised through my research and from interviews with families about creating happy memories with their children.

I – Be nurturing

Being affectionate and caring helps your child's mental well-being through to adulthood. This is supported by a 2007 study in the *Journal of General Practice,* titled 'Childhood Attachment', which states that *'those who are able to form a good attachment with their parents as a child are more able to make good, trusting, and supportive relationships in adulthood.'*

Being nurturing can be demonstrated in many ways, according to Dr Stafford of the Medical Research Council at UCL. Through everyday interactions such as the way you speak with or smile at your child, you are showing you enjoy their company. Spending time with your children does not necessarily need to involve any elaborate gestures or trips to popular resorts, although the exposure is also important for their social development. More importantly, the everyday small gestures can make a big difference. Dr Stafford says:

"We know that if you're able to form a good attachment with your parents when you're a child, you're more able to make good, trusting and supportive relationships later on."

Meghan, the senior executive, shares some insights about how she interacts with her children to cultivate a good relationship over time. She states that she promptly says sorry when in the wrong and, with time, has nurtured a mutually respectful relationship with her children. Over the years, Meghan and her husband have nurtured their children to understand and process their feelings through doing things as a family – such as cycling, sports and exploring different types of foods. Learning and experiencing things together as a family are critical nurturing moments.

While not exhaustive, set out below are some simple, but effective, ways that my husband and I try to nurture happy childhood experiences with our children.

Nurturing through walks

Going for walks with the children, even if it is just to the local supermarket, can be a valuable learning and teaching opportunity to point things out and share information. For example, bike rides with the children when the weather permits is an opportunity to teach road safety which also contributes to their awareness and confidence. Another way to achieve this, depending on the distance to their school, is to aim to walk your child to school when you can. In some

Picture 2: Going for a walk

instances, depending on working and childcare arrangements, it may not be possible to walk daily and perhaps it is necessary to drive to maintain other time commitments. Walking your child to or from school is a great opportunity to talk and share perspectives. This reduces stress levels and increases their happiness according to research published by Amy Packham by *Huffington Post* in 2019. Children who arrive at school less stressed in the morning are more positive about learning and are more likely to perform better.

Nurturing through play

Playing with your child is an opportunity to bond and learn. I use the word 'learn' rather than 'teach', because it will make it more enjoyable if approached from the perspective of a two-way learning experience. It surprises some parents how much they can learn from their children, even if it's just getting to know who their closest friends are, what they think of their teacher and what irks them. This provides useful insight into their character. In my experience, my children enjoy it when their father and I take a keen interest in what is going on in their world, and the latest stories in school.

Although we try as parents to be organised and to plan, there will be times where your child just wants to play outside of the 'play window'. My husband and I have learnt how to manage this over time. For example, instead of telling our children that we are too busy to play or watch them perform an act they have been working on, where practical we'd first pause whatever we are doing and try to join in, even if it is only for a few seconds. Your child will appreciate that you have made the time for them and you will feel better for the break from whatever you were doing, possibly going back to it more refreshed and relaxed. Alternatively, we'd engage for several seconds while advising them to schedule a more appropriate time with no distractions, meaning that they can achieve the desired level of attention.

Other important ways that I play with my children include playing board games, which can lead to improved social skills, strategic and critical thinking, broader vocabulary, better communication, integrity, and developing numeracy skills. Examples of such board games are Monopoly, Articulate, Ludo, Chess, Scrabble, and Snakes and Ladders.

The following story, from a family with two daughters aged eight and six, provides useful insight.

Jane and Ella enjoy role-playing and coming up with dance and gymnastic routines, which they are always keen to perform to their parents. With competing demands, it is not always possible for their parents, Mike and Olivia, to make the time to watch every single show their daughters want to put on at every opportunity. To manage the situation, Olivia suggested that the daughters should design an invitation with a scheduled time, ensuring adequate advance notice for the parents to plan towards so that they can be fully engaged with their performance. This approach proved successful as it eventually led to a new feature in the family's weekly routine, whereby Friday nights became known as show time or movie nights, with popcorn and the necessary treats to make it an enjoyable experience for all. Olivia explains that by following this approach, she and Mike try to spend one or two weekends a month baking with their children when possible. Although she admits she is no Mary Berry, author of the bestselling *Baking Bible*, this gives the family an opportunity to improve their baking skills and to bond, discussing any topics on their children's minds.

Nurturing through chores

When it comes to chores, it initially appears more efficient to complete a task, such as doing the dishes or tidying the laundry, without your child's 'help'. However, involving your child in some domestic chores will also lead to a sense of responsibility as well as making them feel valued.

> "If kids aren't doing the dishes, it means someone else is doing that for them. They're absolved of not only the work, but of learning that work has to be done, and that each one of us must contribute for the betterment of the whole."

This quotation is from Julie Lythcott-Haims, former dean at Stanford University and author of *How to Raise an Adult,* from a *TED Talks* live event. Lythcott-Haims believes that children who do chores go on to become employees who collaborate well with their co-workers, are more empathetic because they understand hard work first hand and are able to take on tasks independently.

During one of the long summer holidays, we had an interesting experience which perhaps highlights how chores could be fun as well as being a good learning opportunity for the children. Our washing machine broke down, but instead

82

Picture 3: Doing chores together

of replacing it with a new one, we decided that as we had only had it a few years, and it is a good brand, we would get it repaired instead. However, it took a few weeks as a number of parts needed to be ordered and could only be installed by the manufacturer's engineers. During this time, my daughter had a party to attend and she asked how the mounting pile of dirty clothes, which included her favourite top that she wanted to wear, would be washed. I replied that we could try to wash it by hand. The look of shock on her face was telling, as she asked, *"How is it possible to wash clothes by hand?"* I laughed and said, *"Don't worry, I will show you."* Still not entirely convinced, she asked, *"How will it get clean and the stains come off?"* I reassured her and showed her how to do it as we attempted to wash by hand in the bath. We turned this into a somewhat fun activity for the day, albeit short-lived.

We were, of course, relieved when the washing machine was repaired later that week. However, this experience gave us some perspective and a deeper appreciation for some amenities, such as a working washing machine, which we previously took for granted.

Nurturing through reading together

Reading together is as much about learning as it is about spending time with your child. Listen to your child read, read to your child and encourage them to take some time out to read alone as well. As children get older it is important to keep this up. In most cases, as confirmed by some of the families in the focus group, reading and continuous learning is a critical leadership trait – leaders are readers.

Picture 4: Reading together

Nurturing through bedroom time

From insights distilled from the best practices shared by the participants in my research, I found that it is valuable for parents to spend time in their children's rooms regularly, as the opportunity provides some insight into their developing personalities. Even as little as one to five minutes in your child's bedroom daily while he or she plays, reads or tidies up, can provide useful insight, and the opportunity for some regular one-to-one time. These little moments can make a positive impact and a big difference over time.

Whenever I am in my children's bedrooms, I use the opportunity to: help them tidy up their rooms and be more organised; just lie on their beds and cuddle them; discuss their day or anything that is bothering them.

Picture 5: Having a lie-in

Some of the families shared that they have a lie-in occasionally during the weekends, cuddling up with their children, and perhaps just listening to soft gospel or classical music, which can be relaxing, and a nice change in rhythm to the weekday rush.

Nurturing through communication

Scheduling family mealtimes as regularly as possible (without any devices) to engage in conversations is a good opportunity to connect with each other properly. For example, enquiring about your child's day, asking what was the best and worst thing about their day, anything new they learnt, who or what made them laugh or annoyed them, really gives an insight into their emotional and social well-being. It also provides the opportunity to offer an alternative,

Picture 6: Family mealtimes

more balanced perspective on a matter. Listed below are some of the questions that some of the parents shared that they typically ask their children several times a week:

- Tell me about your day
- What interesting thing happened?
- Who was on your lunch table?
- Who is best friends with whom now?
- Who is not talking to whom and why?
- How was it in class?
- Did you have any tests, and do you think you did your best?

In some instances, some families may need to leave it until the end of the week to have such open discussions about each other's respective experiences that week. Nonetheless, using any opportunity to discuss and feedback on what could be improved to make life easier for each other or those they interact with is valuable.

Nurturing through laughter

Laughing with another person has been scientifically proven to strengthen the relationship between both parties. For example, sharing jokes, funny stories or just having a quick tickle will contribute to overall better well-being for both the parent and the child.

With time, we have learnt to make time to have a laugh. For example, at the weekends or during the school holidays my children and I enjoy taking 'selfies' and goofing around. We will record funny videos and play them back just to laugh at ourselves. It is important that children learn to laugh at

Picture 7: Laughing and goofing with children

themselves and not take themselves too seriously all the time from a young age. There is, of course, a balance to this as there is a time to be serious when the occasion demands. Some of the most charming and pleasant people I have come across are those who are comfortable in their skin, self-aware, empathetic and can laugh at themselves.

Nurturing through affection

Understandably, it may not always be possible during the morning rush, but cuddling and kissing your child goodbye in the morning can be reassuring for them. In my case, I usually say a little prayer as I kiss them goodbye – as simple as, *"God bless and protect you, darling. Have a lovely day."* An article by Samantha Rodman, clinical psychologist and mum of three, published by the *Business Insider*, states that couples who

Picture 8: Being affectionate

kiss hello and goodbye are happier, and the same principle can be applied to children. Another tip I came across a few years ago that I've sometimes used is to leave 'love notes'. A simple post-it note with the words, 'I love you', 'smile, you're special', can really brighten your child's face and make them feel loved when they later find it hidden in their lunch box, under their pillow, in their pocket or anywhere else.

II – Develop empathy

Thinking about the world as a pyramid, it is sometimes claimed that people who start at the top may not have empathy for those further down, whereas people who start at the bottom and eventually end up at the top are more likely to look down now and again to reach out and pull someone up. Irrespective of the parents' socioeconomic class, children should be nurtured to develop a sense of empathy and kindness.

The findings from the young adults from the focus group suggest that a lot of their success is down to the parents' nurturing. Some of these participants believe that they would have gone off track had it not been for the focused, consistent and deliberate nurturing they received from their parents – be it a two-parent or single-parent home. The young adults strongly believe their parents played a significant role in helping them to discover their path and to get on the right trajectory. Although these young adults who are of the millennial generation do not necessarily think their parents got it perfectly right, they do, however, believe that their parents did the best with the information they had, to ensure the best start and platform. Demonstrating such understanding and empathy is warm and endearing.

III – Encourage independence

According to a study published in the *Journal of Positive Psychology*, referenced in the previous section, psychologically controlling parents can affect their child's happiness well into adulthood. According to Dr Stafford, a psychologist from UCL, a reminder of the examples of psychological control are: being over-protective, overly controlling through invading your child's privacy and trying to make them dependent on you as a parent. This psychological control can mean your child suppresses their emotions or does not know how to regulate or express their emotions as they get older.

Chartered psychologist Dr Lynne Jordan shares some things children need to see their parents do to feel loved, published in the *Journal of Positive Psychology*; these include:

- Daily one-on-one time
- Setting boundaries
- Playing

Summarised below are additional tips from my research to help children develop independence and be happier.

Strategically disrupt their comfort zone

A way of nurturing children to develop independence is through encouraging them out of their comfort zone. I recall an occasion at a conference with my daughter, who was nine years old at the time. I noticed she seemed apprehensive about even just going to the nearby loos by herself. As it was a secure venue, I encouraged her to visit one of the stalls upstairs by herself to pick up a snack, which she did apprehensively. However, I decided to follow behind without her seeing me. When I caught up with her and asked her how she felt, she stated that she was just trying to hurry and return as soon as possible. However, she felt relieved I'd followed her. The next statement she made was critical – *"Next time I think I'll be fine as it won't seem as scary as it was this first time."* Typically, the first time we try something new is always the scariest, being in unchartered territory, where everything looks or feels unfamiliar, your mouth feels dry, stomach feels tight and it takes a lot of courage. However, the next time feels less uneasy until eventually it becomes second nature.

IV – Set boundaries

Feedback from parents from the focus group has shown that household rules and boundaries will help your child to become more independent. Although children often complain and try to breach boundaries, it actually helps them feel reassured. The following story about a discovery by sociologists and psychologists several years ago best illustrates this point.

Contemporary thought assumed that putting up fences around playgrounds made children feel restricted in their recreation. It was then decided to remove the fences so

Picture 9: Discipline

children wouldn't feel confined. Interestingly, the experts found that the opposite effect occurred – children became more inhibited in their activities. They instead huddled towards the middle of the playground and exhibited signs of insecurity. However, when the fences were replaced, the children once more played with great enthusiasm and freedom. The lesson here is we all need boundaries to help define the limits of safety and security. Whereas the 'experts' initially theorised that boundaries restricted creativity, children on the playground proved that we need a clear understanding of what's safe and acceptable for ingenuity to flourish. Therefore, homes will function better when guidelines are clearly communicated, and the consequences for not following them are also completely understood.

A consistent routine that sets out the expectations ensures stability. However, due to work and life pressures, ensuring that our children are well behaved can be very challenging. As a result, parents have resorted to some unorthodox ways in order to achieve the desired behaviours from their children. Set out below are some of these common mistakes, and tips on avoiding them, according to Elizabeth O'Shea, a UK-based parenting expert and director of Parent 4 Success.

Common mistakes and solutions

Bribe

When your child is misbehaving in a shop and you offer them a treat to behave, this sends a mixed message. According to O'Shea, *"Bribery is something you do when your child has started to* misbehave, in order to get them to behave well. A reward is something you offer a child, if they remember to behave well, but before there has been any bad behaviour. If you bribe a child when they are misbehaving, the child sees it as a reward for the bad behaviour."

Solution: Instead of offering the bribe while they are misbehaving, instead reverse the situation by saying that they will receive the gift later if they behave.

Shouting
As parents, sometimes we shout when we are overwhelmed and feel like we do not have control of the situation. However, shouting is not a solution as it creates tension. Although children may appear to initially respond to shouting, it does not work in the long run as you are essentially just forcing your child to behave in that moment.

Solution: A better idea is to have clear rules of what you expect from your child and talk to them in a calm, positive way. It's easier said than done, but this becomes easier with time as the expectations become established.

Inconsistency
Being inconsistent with household rules is something most parents are guilty of. I find that due to competing demands and the general semi-permanent state of fatigue, for example, one week you may focus on your child tidying up their bedroom but the following week you do not because you are too tired to deal with it. This inconsistency may confuse your child about what is expected.

Solution: Consistently reinforce the rules. Additionally, it means that your child grows up understanding the importance of being consistent. In later life, they will be able to apply these skills in maintaining a high standard, when it requires working late on an essay at university or to finish a report for work.

Being authoritarian

Involving children from age five or above in setting the household rules will not only empower them but also contribute to their leadership development from an early age. According to O'Shea, co-setting the rules rather than always dictating them, means children are more engaged and are more likely to cooperate with the 'house rules' they have helped to set.

Solution: O'Shea recommends that getting the family together to determine the solution for reducing the level of shouting, for example, and get the mornings to go smoothly, will result in a mutually agreed set of rules that clearly sets out the expectations for everyone.

Comparing your children to each other

Although this was covered earlier in Chapter 2, it is reiterated here because of the impact of this common misdemeanour that most people are guilty of. In the same way that we would not appreciate it, children also feel frustrated when they are constantly compared to their 'superstar' sibling.

Solution: Rather than comparing your children, instead find the time to talk when things are calmer. Additionally, you could ask your child what positive qualities they see in their sibling, how they can emulate those positive characteristics and vice versa. Ask them and help them to list their positive qualities and how they can help their siblings to improve in those areas.

V – Get to know your child's friends

Several of the parents in my study shared about the importance of getting to know their children's friends and their parents. Children spend a lot of time in school with their friends and it is important to be reassured. Organising playdates doesn't only show how much you care but also helps to develop your child's social skills. Recognising these early friendships and creating opportunities for children to play together as appropriate, encourages the development of key social skills such as teamwork, sharing, trust and independence.

VI – Eating well and exercise

It can sometimes be a challenge to strike the right balance between ensuring a nutritionally balanced diet and your child eating at all. On some days, just getting your child to eat feels like an achievement. Good advice such as ensuring a balanced diet and 60 minutes of physical activity a day to protect children from a host of chronic diseases later, may not always be practical. Even the most health-conscious parent has to compete against a plethora of unhealthy temptations.

Over the years, I have tried to be more organised in this area by designing a meal plan for the week ahead and batch cooking to ensure some nutritional balance. This also enables me to ensure the required grocery items are bought ahead of time and not realising at the last minute that some of the required ingredients have run out. Wellness-coaching experts give parents three rules for healthy eating: make it a family affair, stay involved and keep it simple. Other tips to help busy parents and their children make physical activity and good nutrition a part of the family's everyday life are:

- Plan for healthy meals – for example, we started off by including salad for dinner in the weekly meal at least once a week, and over time it has become more frequent.
- Get children involved and make it fun. For example, at the weekends we blend some of the leftover fruits to make different-flavoured fruit smoothies.
- Weekly sports – we ensure the children are involved in a number of different sports clubs in school, which helps to achieve the balance of physical activities.

Although children do not always enjoy eating their green vegetables, the key is to persevere with the nutritious food and physical activity in family routines, reminding them of the benefits. For example, my four-year-old at the time of writing always asks, whenever he sees vegetables on his plate, what these particular vegetables are good for. Sometimes I may respond, it will make you taller or give you bigger muscles, which then motivates him to eat. Additionally, over

time, my children have learnt that if they eat their greens and
fruits they are more likely to have their preferred snacks.

VII – Instil structure and consistency

A regular bedtime for children could be the key to good
behaviour, according to LiveScience research.

> "Sleep is one of the most important things you can do for a
> child's health and behaviour."

Dr Carolyn D'Ambrosio

This study also found that:

> "Children who don't have a regular bedtime behave worse
> than those who go to sleep at the same time each night."

> "Seven-year-olds who had inconsistent bedtimes were
> more hyperactive with more social, emotional and conduct
> problems, than their better-rested peers."

The results revealed that these behavioural problems grew
worse the more years a child spent without a consistent
bedtime. The reason for this is that children who do not
get enough good sleep may not be as easy-going as they are
more likely to be irritable. From a neurological perspective,
insufficient sleep inhibits the development of pathways
between neurons in the brain. According to Dean Beebe,

director of the neuropsychology programme at Cincinnati Children's Hospital Medical Center:

> "We're talking about a brain that is constantly remodelling through early childhood, with connections being strengthened and weakened."

In the study, researchers looked at data from more than 10,000 babies born in the UK in 2001 and 2002. The findings clearly showed an association between children behaving better and a regular bedtime. Having an irregular sleep schedule had the greatest effect on a child's behaviour and those with later bedtimes also tended to behave worse. A lack of sleep also shows up in a child's school performance, mood, eating habits and behaviour. Therefore, having bedtime routines and a regular bedtime adds structure and consistency to a child's schedule; it helps them perform their best the next day and thus makes for a happier child. Consistent and early bedtimes means that children get enough rest to get through all stages of sleep, each of which have important functions that regulate the body according to the study by the Sleep Foundation. For example, deep sleep helps people to wake up feeling refreshed, while REM (rapid eye movement) sleep helps to improve memory skills, according to Dr Carolyn D'Ambrosio, director of the sleep centre at Tufts Medical Center and the Floating Hospital for Children in Boston. She also recommends that parents start the process of regular bedtimes early in a child's life. However, even for a late starter, the good news is that the introduction of a more structured bedtime will lead to significant improvements. Children can perceive and prepare for bedtime by beginning their nightly routines, such as brushing teeth, bathing, putting on pyjamas, reading a story and limiting stimulating distractions from a TV or devices. Although this may not work every day, the key is to be persistent and consistent even on weekends and during the holidays.

Set out below are the recommended hours of sleep, at different ages, by the National Sleep Foundation.

Age	Recommended	May be appropriate	Not recommended
Newborns 0–3 months	14 to 17 hours	11 to 13 hours 18 to 19 hours	Less than 11 hours More than 19 hours
Infants 4–11 months	12 to 15 hours	10 to 11 hours 16 to 18 hours	Less than 10 hours More than 18 hours
Toddlers 1–2 years	11 to 14 hours	9 to 10 hours 15 to 16 hours	Less than 9 hours More than 16 hours
Pre-schoolers 3–5 years	10 to 13 hours	8 to 9 hours 14 hours	Less than 8 hours More than 14 hours
School-aged children 6–13 years	9 to 11 hours	7 to 8 hours 12 hours	Less than 7 hours More than 12 hours
Teenagers 14–17 years	8 to 10 hours	7 hours 11 hours	Less than 7 hours More than 11 hours
Young adults 18–25 years	7 to 9 hours	6 hours 10 to 11 hours	Less than 6 hours More than 11 hours
Adults 26–64 years	7 to 9 hours	6 hours 10 hours	Less than 6 hours More than 10 hours
Older adults ≥65 years	7 to 8 hours	5 to 6 hours 9 hours	Less than 5 hours More than 9 hours

Table 3: Recommended hours of sleep by the National Sleep Foundation

Most parents found this table to be useful, especially in the early years, for ensuring their children get enough sleep. For example, I made sure my children had a nap for approximately an hour daily until the age of four. Regular afternoon naps provide some respite for parents and children wake up refreshed, thus leading to better temperaments all round and the added benefit of higher cognitive development at a critical phase.

VIII – Teach niceness

Getting the best out of people is about empathy, feelings, and acknowledgement. On some level, we are all driven by how we feel and how we are perceived. According to Maya Angelou, a poet and civil rights activist, 'people never forget how you made them feel'. There is great reward in being nice and treating people well, irrespective of our differences; treating people with respect, dignity and equity. My husband and I make a point to remind our children to always be nice, for example, not to join in if anyone is being treated bad and to instead find a way to support the person being picked on or encourage everyone else to try to be nice instead. We will say to our children from time to time to look out for anyone who looks left out or doesn't seem to have a friend and try to be nice to them. It was heartwarming one year when my daughter invited someone to her birthday play date whose name I didn't recognise from previous events or from discussions. She said that she'd invited this new friend who'd recently joined the school mid year as this will help the new pupil make more friends and settle in quicker. This is something we can never teach our children enough of, not just by telling them but also from modelling it ourselves, what they observe of how we treat people, what we say in their presence as well as their absence. Our children are watching and listening to us all the time, even when it doesn't look like it.

SUMMARY: RAISING A HAPPIER CHILD

1. Be nurturing
    Being affectionate and not psychologically controlling
    helps your child's well-being through to adulthood. Some
    ways to be nurturing are to:

    *   Go for walks
    *   Play and laugh together
    *   Assign chores
    *   Read together
    *   Spend time in your child's bedroom
    *   Communicate with your children regularly and
        openly
    *   Be affectionate

2. Develop empathy

3. Encourage independence

4. Set boundaries, avoiding the following mistakes:

    *   Bribing
    *   Shouting
    *   Being inconsistent
    *   Being authoritarian
    *   Comparing your children

5. Get to know your children's friends and their parents

6. Eat well and exercise

    - Plan for healthy meals
    - Get the children involved and make it fun
    - Sign up to after-school physical activities clubs

7. Structure and consistency

    - Set regular bedtimes – sleep is one of the most important things you can do for a child's health and behaviour as *'children who don't have a regular bedtime behave worse than children who go to sleep at a regular time each night'*
    - Start bedtime routines early in your child's life and ensure they get enough sleep every day
    - Maintain consistent bedtime routines, even on weekends and during the school holidays

8. Teach niceness

CHAPTER 7

Financial Intelligence Quotient (FiQ)

In Chapter 1, we discussed the importance of IQ, which stands for intelligence quotient; it is essentially a standardised test designed to measure innate human intelligence and analytical ability. Emotional quotient (EQ) as also discussed earlier, is the ability to navigate social complexities and make personal decisions that yield positive results. Up until now, the importance of having the right combination of IQ versus EQ has been articulated in numerous ways. In this chapter, I offer a third component, which I will call Financial Intelligence Quotient (FiQ), loosely defined as the ability to understand how money works and how to build personal wealth. I believe that FiQ is complementary to IQ and EQ, for a more rounded person with financial stability. Starting with IQ forming the first component, with EQ as the second component,

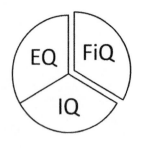

FiQ is the third component. EQ is appropriately the second component, as the ability to manage yourself and people may enhance the outcomes from your IQ, and positively improve your FiQ. There is some degree of interdependency between these components though not necessarily a correlation. I started with IQ as that's inherent, while EQ and FiQ can be nurtured over time.

Daniel Goleman's *Emotional Intelligence* helped me to focus on developing my emotional intelligence and become more self-aware from an early age. However, author Robert T. Kiyosaki's bestseller *Rich Dad Poor Dad* significantly improved my FiQ, as my financial literacy skills developed rapidly after reading this book. Kiyosaki discusses the difference between the statements: '*I cannot afford it*' compared to '*How can I afford it?*' The second statement opens up our minds to think of possibilities, lifting limits and opening up our creative ability to think systematically and strategically about how to achieve the desired result. I purchased my first property in my late teens by applying this same concept. Although the idea to buy a property in the first place came from my mentor and spiritual father, this approach to solving problems has enabled me to achieve a lot more than I would have otherwise. Thinking, 'how can I solve this challenge?', 'how can I help my children maximise their potential?', 'how can I help my daughter be successful in her athletics trials?', resulted in developing a methodical and strategic plan towards the desired outcomes each time. I shared the story in the early chapters of this book about how we worked together to help my daughter get into the school athletics team. First, we found out which activities formed part of the trials and then asked her which she was weakest in. Through teamwork, with her father taking her along on his daily jogs and the additional practice at home in the garden, she did better than she would have otherwise and made the team, albeit the reserve team initially. However, she went on to become a critical member of the first team covering almost all sports in later years.

Financial literacy is defined as the ability to understand and manage financial resources properly. An OECD (Organisation for Economic Co-operation and Development) study, published in 2017, about young people's grasp of money issues around the world, found that only 12% of 15-year-olds correctly answered the financial literacy questions. The study used the same PISA (Programme for International Student Assessment) scoring system that ranks abilities in reading and maths. PISA aims to evaluate education systems worldwide. This result served as a wake-up call, not just for parents and schools but also for regulators. The OECD is an organisation that provides a forum for governments to promote policies that will improve the economic and social well-being of people around the world. The study explored students' experience and knowledge of money, providing an overall picture of 15-year-olds' ability in real-life situations involving financial issues and decisions. The UK did not take part in this PISA test, though financial literacy education became part of the national curriculum for the first time in September 2014, for Key Stages 3 and 4 (ages 11–16). Some studies show that there are still challenges in this area, as not all primary schools have the resources for this.

According to a research article published by the *Money Charity* on financial education in 2016, parents have the primary responsibility for teaching their children financial literacy. Two thirds of teachers believe that a mix of both training and delivery from outside experts will help schools develop the skills to deliver financial education objectives.

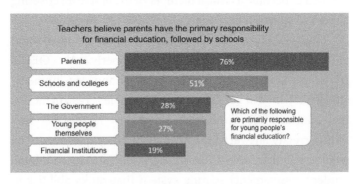

Figure 4: Responsibility for teaching financial literacy
Source: Money Charity

The chart above shows the results of a survey completed by teachers about who they believe has the responsibility for teaching financial education. As can be seen, 76% of teachers believe that parents have the primary responsibility for this.

In this chapter, I provide some basic examples to help

parents teach their children financial literacy from early on at home. The aim is to help children to grow up with the life skills, knowledge and confidence they need to successfully earn and manage money by increasing their awareness.

I – Understanding and handling money

By the age of four, many children understand that money can be exchanged for something they want or need. Playing games that stimulate financial thinking is a good way to teach children about money matters. For example, games like Monopoly introduce money management, property ownership, spending within your means and calculating simple arithmetic. My four-year-old plays a trading game with his sisters that has developed his awareness of the value of items and when a trade or transaction seems inconsistent (or, in his words, a 'scam' or 'rubbish trade') in the value exchanged. The objective is that the skills children learn from playing these games will translate seamlessly into real-world applications. This can also lead to some fun and quality bonding time (albeit competitive) when parents join in.

A 2013 University of Cambridge piece of research from behaviour experts David Whitebread and Sue Bingham found that children form money habits by the age of seven from their parents. Good financial literacy and approach to money, such as planning ahead and delaying gratification, can avoid problems later on. By teaching your children about money, you help them discover the relationship of earning to spending and saving. This way, children begin to understand the value of money. A

TedX event with David McQueen, entrepreneur, professional speaker and executive coach, titled *Education Beyond Schooling*, stated that, from his over 30 years' experience within the education sector, a key education is financial education, which is missing in school curriculums. McQueen discussed the importance of teaching children to be more curious about the world around them, as well as the importance of financial literacy, the difference between asset and liability, and learning to be entrepreneurial. He advocates the importance of teaching children about money, although this should not be left to the schools alone. Education is not about passing tests but learning, developing a sense of curiosity and aspiration. For example, your child should understand why they should perhaps own Nike stocks before asking you to buy them Huaraches (a popular range of Nike trainers at the time of writing). With the appropriate focus and nurturing, the financial awareness and entrepreneurial acumen will develop over time. However, according to Guy Shore, former research director for the UK government's *Money Advice* Service, the window is zero to seven, suggesting that 'it's very hard to reverse those habits later in life'. However, if you miss this window it doesn't mean your child is destined to a life of financial struggles. It does, however, mean it will be a challenge to change later on. This is why I recommend starting as early as possible.

Simple financial lessons between ages three to five are:

• Waiting to buy something you want.

A 40-year research project at Stanford University has found that delayed gratification is the one quality that can predict if people will be successful or not. In

fact, this Stanford research found that children who are willing to delay gratification have higher test scores, better social skills, better responses to stress and lower levels of substance abuse. This research, based on the Marshmallow Test, is discussed at the end of this chapter.
- Learning to save for what you want.

    For example, piggy banks to save birthday monetary gifts.

The definitions provided below are to help children understand how money plays an important part of our daily lives.

Term	Definition
Budget	A budget is the amount of money that you have available to spend; you can buy something less than the amount, but you cannot exceed it.
Money	Money is used to buy something you want or need. This can be in the form of coins, notes or 'money cards' (the difference between debit and credit cards could be taught later).
Mortgage	Parents sometimes borrow money from the bank to buy a house. This is known as getting a mortgage. Parents then pay back the mortgage, little by little from their wages, every month until it is all paid off. Sometimes it takes up to 25 years to pay back all the money borrowed from the bank.
Taxes	Every month before parents receive their wages, tax is taken out. The tax is the money the governments use to pay for hospitals, roads, police and more, for a safer community.
Wages	Parents go to work to earn some money called wages or salary.

Table 4: Early financial terms

EXAMPLE EXERCISE: UNDERSTANDING THE LINK BETWEEN WAGES, MORTGAGE AND SAVING THE DIFFERENCE

Money

- Parents earn money when they go to work, known as wages or salary.
- Children can also earn some money by doing chores around the house, known as pocket money.
- The key learning here is that people normally need to work to earn money.

Tax

- Some parents pay 20% tax or more.
- Children can give 10% towards charitable causes from pocket money or birthday monetary gifts.

Saving

- From the money received after tax is taken away, known as the net salary, parents pay for rent or mortgage, buy food, pay bills like electricity, heating and water. What remains could then be saved, or sometimes used to pay for things like birthdays, Christmas presents, a car, holidays, etc.

Example

	£
Wages	1,000
Tax	– 200
Net salary	800
Mortgage	– 400
Food	– 120
Light, heating	– 80
Water	– 30
Remaining balance	170

The money remaining can go towards the savings, other expenses or for an emergency.

Further takeaways to communicate to children

- The more money that can be saved each month, the bigger the presents and holidays.

Exercise

- Ask your children if they can think of things the members of the family could all do to try to save money.
- Answers could be along the lines of – "*Switch lights off, not keep taps running and not waste food, so that parents can save more.*"

II – Budgeting

A simple way of teaching budgeting is, for example, when we go to a convenience or express grocery store. Almost every time I take the children out, as most parents can identify with, children typically ask for treats. On one occasion, I told them that their budget was £1 each, and my six-year-old at the time asked, "Mummy, what's a budget?" to which I replied:

> "A budget is the amount of money that you have available to spend; you can buy something less than the amount, but not more than your budget."

This has been useful because it means that whenever we go to a shop, the first question they typically ask is about their budget. In most cases, I advise them that the budget is zero. This manages their expectations from the outset. Sometimes, they ask if they can buy something using some of their savings from their piggy bank if their choice exceeds their budget, or on the occasions when the budget is zero. I find that this is also useful to help them develop discipline and not to expect treats every time they accompany me to the shops.

See the detailed example of a budgeting exercise. The same exercise can be conducted with different budgets. For example, with a £40 budget, the children could afford a picnic in the local park and still have just as much fun.

EXAMPLE: BIRTHDAY BUDGET AND PLANNING

Alex is turning seven and she wants to have a party. Her parents have advised that the budget for her birthday celebrations is £200 and suggested the following two options.

1. Option 1: Have an all-inclusive birthday party at the local play centre for:

- £14 per child (goody bag, food and drinks included)
- £40 for personalised cake

2. Option 2: Arrange a playdate at home with the following associated costs:

- Party entertainer for £100 (inclusive of mini awards for up to 15 friends) or no entertainer
- Pizzas for £40
- Drinks and snacks £20
- £40 for personalised cake

Additional information:

- No more than 15 children
- Minimum of ten children with option 1
- Budget excludes birthday gift which will be bought separately
- Party bags are £3 each

Using the above information, Alex spent a few days after school and part of a weekend working through the different options to determine which would enable her to invite the highest number of friends and still save money for a small toy.

Exercise

Can you provide some pointers and assistance in working through both options?

Sample answers and considerations below when we tried this with my daughter.

First iteration

- Option 1 – with this option she worked out that she could only invite 11 people. This did not initially appeal to her because she had drawn up a list of 15 names.
- Option 2 – we worked out that she could invite more friends. Not including the cost of an entertainer in her budget would leave more money for party bags and other things that would be used for the entertainment.

Result

After further iterations and some direction and help with calculations, she eventually chose option 1, and suggested that we purchase a cheaper cake instead, one that was not necessarily personalised. This way she was able to invite 12 friends and she thought this option meant she did not need to work so hard tidying up afterwards.

I have shared below some of the questions asked as we worked through the various options over a few days. This gives some insight into the thought process this sort of exercise can generate in young minds.

Follow up questions/statements

- I'll need to invite less people for the budget, or just do a playdate.
- Can we get a cheaper cake?
- Maybe I can have a small playdate at home instead.
- Is there a cheaper venue for the party?
- Can we get cheaper food like just sandwiches and use the rest for lots of sweets?
- Can I borrow some money from my piggy bank?
- If there is money left over from the budget, can I use it to buy more toys instead of saving it?

For the last three question above, my response was 'no'. However, my explanation for the response to the last bullet point was that if she saved what was remaining, we could put it towards any holiday trips, nicer new trainers or just save for the future.

Skills learnt: budgeting, saving, arithmetic, strategic thinking, saving, future planning.

Money can be an exciting topic for children, as many are keen to learn about earning, spending and saving money, even at a very young age. Most young children are ready to learn the basic concepts introduced here. This can then be embedded and built on over time through repetition, experience and practice.

As parents, we need to make a conscious effort to teach these concepts to our children, taking advantage of those teachable moments that make it easier for your child to grow up to be a financially literate and responsible adult.

III – Delayed Gratification: The Marshmallow Test

In the 1960s, a Stanford professor named Walter Mischel and his team conducted a series of psychological tests on hundreds of children – most of them around the ages of four and five years old – and revealed what is now believed to be one of the most important characteristics for success in health, work and life.

The experiment consisted of bringing each child into a private room, sitting them down and placing a marshmallow on the table in front of them.

The researcher told the child that he was going to leave the room and that if the child did not eat the marshmallow while he was away, then they would be rewarded with a second marshmallow. However, if the child decided to eat the first one before the researcher came back, then they would not get a second marshmallow.

So the choice was: one treat right now or two treats later.

The researcher left the room for 15 minutes. The footage of the children waiting alone in the room was rather entertaining. Some kids jumped up and ate the first marshmallow as soon as the researcher left the room. Others fidgeted in their chairs as they tried to restrain themselves, but eventually gave in to temptation a few minutes later. And finally, a few of the children did manage to wait the entire time.

Published in 1972, however, the most interesting part of this study came years later. The researchers conducted follow up studies and tracked each child's progress in a number of areas as they grew up. The children who were willing to delay gratification and waited to receive the second marshmallow ended up having higher test scores, lower levels of substance abuse, lower likelihood of obesity, better responses to stress, better social skills and generally better scores in a range of other life measures.

The researchers followed each child for more than 40 years, and over and over again, the group who waited patiently for the second marshmallow succeeded in whatever capacity they were measuring. This series of experiments proved that the ability to delay gratification was critical for success in life.

In other words, the child's ability to delay gratification and display self-control was not a predetermined trait, but rather was impacted by the experiences and environment that surrounded them. A subsequent experiment found that just a few minutes of reliable or unreliable experiences were enough to push the actions of each child in one direction or another. The Marshmallow Test is just one piece of data, a small insight into the story of success. One choice a four-year-old makes will not necessarily determine the rest of his or her life.

The key takeaway here is that you can train your child and yourself to become better at delaying gratification, simply by making a few small improvements. In the case of the children in the study, this meant being exposed to a reliable environment: by promising something small and then delivering. Over time this will build trust with your child.

SUMMARY: DEVELOPING FINANCIAL LITERACY

How to develop financial literacy:

1. Understanding and handling money

- Wait to buy
- Wait and save
- Play financial games

2. Budgeting
3. Delayed gratification

Benefits of financial literacy:

- Helps to instil resilience from a young age by challenging children to think logically
- Builds early foundation to develop core skills including problem solving and communication
- Introduces children to an understanding of finance, budgeting and how money works
- Delayed gratification leads to higher test scores, better social skills and better stress management
- Highly interactive and fun. The birthday party planning example is a fun way of teaching financial literacy and teamwork for primary school-aged children.

PART II

Bringing It All Together

"Leaders set high standards. Refuse to tolerate mediocrity or poor performance."

Brian Tracy,
Bestselling Author, American-Canadian Motivational Speaker

CHAPTER 8

Parental Attributes

"Some people are born great while others achieve greatness, and some others have greatness thrust upon 'em."

William Shakespeare

If every parent believed that his or her child would achieve greatness, that child would have a higher chance to achieve it because of the support and encouragement from the parents. However, it will require a strategy to support our children to be happy, stay out of trouble, perform well in school and hopefully lead a successful adult life in the future. A number of the best practices covered in this book discuss the various factors that contribute to achieving this goal. Unsurprisingly, parents are critical to the well-being and success of their children; much of it comes down to the nurturing and mind-set of the parents. For example, Dan Brown, the bestselling author of *The Da Vinci Code*, attributes some of the reasons why his books became bestsellers to some of the pastimes he enjoyed as a child with his parents. Dan Brown's father inadvertently contributed to his success with the code-breaking and treasure hunt games they played together. This has turned out to be a unique selling point in a number of his bestselling books, some of which I have found to be interesting and engaging.

In Clayton Christensen's book titled *How Will You Measure Your Life?*, he gives a comprehensive analysis of why some people appear to be wired with a high need for achievement. However, because he and his wife Christine placed a lot of importance on their family goals, they decided early on to play the long game. According to Christensen, we should allocate resources according to our long-term measure of success, and then apply the discipline to stay aligned by setting boundaries, having perspective and always going back to the big picture.

Over the years, in my career and through life's journey in general, I have observed parents who prioritise work at the expense of spending quality time with their children or being present. Eventually, they feel that they do not recognise what their children have become or realise that no real relationship has developed from their sporadic and inconsistent investment of time with their children through the years. The lesson I draw from this is that, if you put off investing this time during the early years and only focus on building your career instead, you may find that by the time you feel ready to, the game is already over.

Most parents identify with the need to give their children the best opportunities, with each new generation of parents focused on creating possibilities that they themselves wished they had. With the best of intentions these parents start defining the components of their children's village – sometimes consisting of a plethora of coaches and tutors appointed to provide their children with enriching and varying experiences that will make them more rounded. Perhaps this is why you are reading this book. I would like to add a caveat that with everything in life, balance is critical. There are some experiences and exposures that our children need, especially concerning their future happiness, that should not be outsourced. In business, the theory of capabilities provides the framework for the optimal way to outsource – and when it does not make sense to do so. This is an economic theory conceived in the 1980s by economist Amartya Sen and philosopher Martha Nussbaum, as an alternative approach to welfare economics. The core principle of the capability approach is on what individuals are able to do. The same principle applies here.

As parents or practitioners, our early challenges and areas of failure provide some useful insight into the sort of challenges that our children are likely to confront. We can then leverage this insight to help our children prepare for the future. Children should learn to overcome difficult challenges, take on responsibilities and learn to be team players. These opportunities are important for developing critical skills and understanding processes. It is therefore important to check in with your child regularly to ensure they are developing the necessary collaborative and entrepreneurial skills they're being exposed to, and not just going along for the ride.

The danger is despite being exposed to varied experiences, if children are not engaged, they may not develop the desired capabilities that translate into employable or value-adding skills in the future.

Some of the important common parental attributes, distilled from my research and according to a report published by the *Business Insider* for raising more rounded high-performance children are set out below. I am sharing some of the content here for awareness, and also because different parents will find different attributes useful to further complement some of their existing attributes. This is by no means exhaustive, nor intended to be prescriptive.

I – High expectations

The expectations parents have of their children plays a big role in attainment, according to research by the University of California's professor Neal Halfon, summarised as follows:

> "Parents who saw university in their child's future seemed to manage their child towards that goal, irrespective of their income and other assets."

In essence, you are more likely to achieve what you have envisioned. This falls in line with another finding called the Pygmalion effect, which states, *"What one person expects of another can come to serve as a self-fulfilling prophecy."* This theory suggests that children can live up to their parents' expectations as well as their own.

Pygmalion was a Greek mythological figure who fell in love with a statue he created, which then came to life. Social psychologist Robert Rosenthal and his co-author Lenore Jacobson coined the term to describe the findings of a 1965 experiment in a California school. Students took a test to identify those with higher academic ability. Teachers were then given the names of pupils supposedly identified as having a higher ability. As expected, these students showed a significantly higher performance over their classmates when tested again at the end of the year. However, the catch is that this special group of students were chosen at random. The only difference between them and their peers, according to the psychologists, 'was in the mind'. This further supports the idea that the expectations held about our children can make an enormous difference in how they perform. Therefore, as parents, it is imperative that we support our children to maximise their potential by having positive expectations, as they develop their awareness of the impact of perception so that they learn to present their most authentic selves.

II – Healthy relationship between parents

A review by the University of Illinois found that children raised in high-conflict families appeared to fare worse than children of parents with a healthy relationship. Some of the impact of this extended even into their twenties. This is a critical point, to ensure that as parents we make a conscious effort to create a happy environment for our children to enable them to achieve their potential. Although it is inevitable to occasionally have some degree of disagreement and tension in any relationship, the key is to have adequate self-control to ensure that the children are not exposed to an environment that is full of tension.

From personal experience, whenever there is tension between my husband and me, we try to compartmentalise our emotions and function positively in front of our children, with a view to pick up discussions or heated exchange later. This is not always easy to do as there is the tendency to want to deal with issues right away. However, it became easier over time and this proved useful as the passing of time led to a more balanced perspective during discussions later. The key point here is that even in the event that your child does witness a disagreement, it is important that they also witness reconciliation. It is critical as children grow up and build relationships, that they know how to discuss and resolve disagreements constructively, positively and respectfully.

III – Impact of higher education

Academia is not for everyone. There are countless examples of very successful people in society who do not particularly have a high level of academic education. However, a high level of education up to university level can be a form of insurance for a child's future success as an adult. Additionally, through the process of completing their education, they are developing key skills as well as building their social networks through the exposure to new and potentially lasting relationships or future partnerships. The old saying *'it's not what you know but who you know'* is timeless. A number of influential people in society, from politics to business, tend to have been classmates at university or members of some extra-curricular club growing up. In the introduction, I alluded to an interesting article published by *The Guardian*, titled 'PPE: the Oxford degree that runs Britain'. The article discusses how Oxford University graduates in philosophy, politics and economics represent a significant proportion of Britain's elite, more than any other course at any other university. *"From the right to the left, there have been successive networks of 'PPEists' in all levels of British politics, since the degree was established 97 years ago. It is overwhelmingly from Oxford that the governing elite has reproduced itself, generation after generation"*, according to the British political biographer John Campbell. This is perhaps why a lot of people in Whitehall or Capitol Hill arrive with a lot of social capital, developed over time through their networks. The term 'social capital' describes the intangible resources of community and trust upon which people can draw some benefits. In other words, your networks and relationships that contribute to your influence and social status.

According to the University of Michigan's psychologist Sandra Tang mothers who finished secondary school or university were more likely to raise children that did the same. Aspiration is at least partially responsible, as supported by another study from Bowling Green State University psychologist Eric Dubow, which found that:

> "Parents' educational level when the child was eight years old, significantly predicted educational and occupational success for the child 40 years later."

Parental educational level appears to be an important predictor of children's educational and behavioural outcomes, although there are some exceptions to this. There are countless examples where parents with lesser educational attainment have nurtured their children to achieve more. Because of some of the perceived shortcomings and limitations experienced by the parents, they try to turn this around for their children, seeking out and creating opportunities for them that they wish they'd had.

The perception that students from less affluent households perform less well in school on average compared to their more privileged peers is not a new phenomenon. A letter from Tony Wagner, author of *Creating Innovators: The Making of Young People Who Will Change the World*, to business leaders stated that data from the National Assessment for Educational Progress found that '*over 40% of the variation in average reading scores, and 46% of the variation in average math scores is associated with variation in how affluent a child's background is*'.

This is supported by the chart by author Dan Pink illustrated in Figure 5. On the horizontal axis is family income, and on the vertical axis the average SAT score for students from families in each group. It seems that the higher the parents' income, the higher their children's SAT scores.

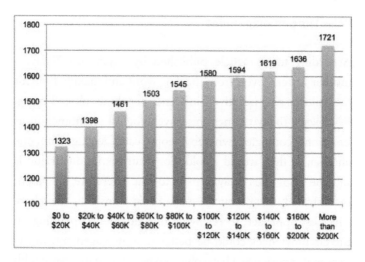

Figure 5: SAT scores versus parental income
Source: Daniel H. Pink

This is not an exact science, as there will be anomalies, with students scoring high despite being from low-income groups and vice versa, but the point here is that parents with more disposable income are more able to provide the resources to support and prepare their children to perform better at exams.

Although there are various policies and laws that could be implemented to reduce this gap, the specifics of this are out of the scope of this book. This information has been shared here for awareness and completeness, with the purpose of setting out some of the parental attributes that contribute to the overall picture.

IV – Time management

According to an article published by *Psychology Today*, a mother's stress levels from juggling work and making time for the children may negatively influence her children's well-being. *Psychology Today* defines this psychological phenomenon as 'emotional contagion', whereby people 'catch' feelings from one another, as they would a cold. For example, if your friend is sad, the gloominess may transfer to you. Therefore, if a parent is frustrated, this emotional state could transfer to the child. The best approach to resolving this situation depending on the circumstances could be better time management. In my personal experience, I have phases where I have the bandwidth to get involved in various projects, and other times I carve out time to achieve a better work-life balance for the family. I have learnt from friends and family with very busy schedules, the benefits of outsourcing some domestic chores in order to spend quality time nurturing the children instead. This has resulted in more time created and less stress. For example, when my children were much younger, I occasionally employed a cleaner at busy times to top up the cleaning effort. It took me some time to become comfortable with this arrangement without feeling guilty or somehow inadequate for outsourcing some of the cleaning. However, I realised that at the end of the day I was making the best of the time available and maximising the quality time spent nurturing the family. This enabled us to be more productive overall, freeing up more time to spend on personal projects. At the start, I would try to tidy up before the cleaner arrived so that she would not think I was untidy or lazy. With the passing of time I felt less and less guilty about having the cleaner come in to help. However, as the children got older and as I achieved a better work-life balance, I no longer feel the need to outsource any of the cleaning at the time of writing.

Make chores fun

A good example of making chores less tedious is with the ironing, which a lot of parents may relate to. I would typically plan it around catching up on any TV boxsets of my favourite programmes. I remember my aunt came to visit once; let us call her Grace. One evening as we all caught up about our respective days, watching the news or any interesting programmes on TV, Aunt Grace observed as I set up the ironing station in such a way so that I could still engage with the conversation as well as watch TV with everyone else. She said that was a genius moment for her as it brought back memories of how she never used to look forward to doing the ironing when her children were growing up, as it was always in the laundry or utility room and a boring experience. Aunt Grace commented on how such a simple concept of doing the ironing while sitting down comfortably and watching a favourite programme appeared to have revolutionised the experience, which would otherwise have been considered mundane. Perhaps this was something to do with my aunt's generation. I suspect that most people currently do this now instinctively, and am sharing here for broader awareness just in case.

Online groceries

Doing the weekly grocery shopping online has contributed to helping parents manage their time better. In my experience, it takes me less than ten minutes every week and I can do it at anytime from anywhere. This saves me up to 90 minutes every week, as I do not have to drive to the supermarket, worry about parking or the size of the shopping. However, I do try to go to the supermarket occasionally, just to see what is new and to keep in touch. I also aim to take the children with me on occasions as part of the learning experience.

Take the time you find

I find that in order to achieve my various goals I've learnt to 'take what I can get'. Sometimes, I find that if I wait for a scheduled time to do something, such as getting in touch with someone, reading, tidying up or even writing, I may never find the perfect block of time required to start and finish the task. However, using the odd ten minutes here and there can be effective in chipping away at a mammoth task list. Using the small pockets of time, even just being able to start a task and stop in exactly ten minutes with the view to return later when I have more time, can be very effective. I find that this makes the process less arduous and doing chores in little chunks at a time makes even the biggest tasks more manageable.

Other times I practise the concept of 'do as you go'. If I walk past a mess or something out of place, I try to tidy that little section up there and then. That way there's less of a build-up.

Make time to 'do almost nothing'

At least once a week I try to get up about an hour before the children wake up. I use this time to sometimes catch up on the post, do some reading or plan for the week ahead. Other times I just sit and do nothing in order to regain some sanity. I reflect and think about the day or week ahead with a cup of tea in hand. I learnt this principle from Warren Buffett, one of the world's most successful investors. Buffett apparently creates a lot of free time in his weekly schedule. This philosophy has created one of the world's most successful business records in history, because he creates time to think.

V – Working mothers

According to a study by Harvard Business School, there are significant benefits for children growing up with mothers who work outside the home. The study found that daughters of working mothers were 23% more likely to attain higher education, were more likely to have a job in a supervisory role and earnt more money compared to their peers raised by stay-at-home mothers. The sons of working mothers also tended to contribute more with household chores and childcare later, when they have a family. Specifically, the study found that these group of men spent seven and a half more hours a week on childcare and 25 more minutes on housework.

Through my research, I learnt that in some cultures even if the mothers choose to stay at home, there is emphasis on the mothers being highly skilled, as they have a significant influence in how children develop, how their characters and personalities form. I have had conversations with mothers who feel that their degree is wasted as 'stay-at-home' mothers. I share this perspective to try to encourage them otherwise, to instead recognise that their degree, and the time at university developing various skills, is actually very critical to how they nurture and help shape their children's mind-set. Additionally, it means that they can apply their knowledge and judgement to guide and motivate their children should they face certain challenges later on.

Economic pressures on the family causing both parents to work long hours, leaving children to their own devices with TV or social media as babysitters, means that even for well-intentioned parents the opportunity cost of the daily nurturing interactions between parent and child that build emotional stability and competences can be enormous if left unchecked. The resulting deficit inevitably lays the foundation for grave problems, if corrective or preventative measures are not taken early to keep more children on track.

Although it is good for mothers to work, in my experience I believe in everything with balance. If parents have the resources and stability such that one parent can either work flexibly or take some time off, especially during the critical foundational early years, that could be beneficial for their children's happiness and well-being. In my case, I always worked full time and it was a challenge to try to be on top of everything and still maintain some sanity. As a result, I took a mini sabbatical when my eldest daughter was eight years old. I had just completed my MBA, having worked intensely in the financial services industry for approximately 14 years full time in fairly senior and demanding roles, at the time of writing. The time off served the family well, as I used the time to recalibrate our schedules, routines and just to be present. I used the opportunity to get to know the children's various personalities better and the challenges they were dealing with during a critical phase of their lives. During this time off, as well as pursuing other personal and business writing projects, I redesigned the dinner menu for a healthier, balanced, nutritious diet for the family. We could all sit for dinner together from around 6.15 p.m. almost every day. I used this mini sabbatical to refresh, re-energise, upskill, network and build relationships that I would not otherwise have been able to, and it was useful in finishing this book. Having said that, even though I had more time than usual in this period, I still had to ensure I managed my time well and declined some engagements by learning how to say, "*Sorry, I can't make it.*" These five little words have such potent qualities that can make the difference between a healthy, stress-free day and a meltdown. Some days when we find ourselves spread thin, having promised to be here or there, we may feel overwhelmed with all the commitments we have made. If we are to have better relationships and healthier lives, I believe we need to become comfortable using these five little words, "*Sorry, I can't make it*". I remember one busy weekend; having worked a full week, so many commitments were inadvertently shunted to the weekend. My to-do list was as follows: I'd promised to visit a friend who'd had a baby and I felt guilty that I hadn't visited yet; another friend had organised a networking event and I promised I'd come along to make up the numbers and for general moral support. Other commitments included agreeing to take my daughter shopping for her upcoming birthday and promising to write a letter of recommendation for another friend applying to complete an MBA programme. Additionally, I am a non-executive director on a board and a quorum was required at the emergency board meeting that was organised at the last minute for that weekend, and I needed to read some reports in preparation. Not to mention, there was some work to do around the house to prepare for a house valuation booked for the upcoming Monday. Somehow, I found that I had agreed to all of these commitments, which were more than enough even in perfectly synchronised conditions. Feeling the pressure to live up to my promises, I set out early to try to accomplish everything on my list for that day – but through the day there were moments I felt impatient and irritable. At the end of the day, I managed to achieve most of the things on the list, but at the cost of not spending much quality time with my children – even being impatient with them at times. Essentially, with this feeling of guilt, I did not really feel like I had achieved much that day. In hindsight, I wish I'd said, *"Sorry, I can't make it"* to at least one or two of the commitments on my list. Although one or two people may have felt disappointed for a moment, they would have understood and appreciated the fact that sometimes we need to pace ourselves for better mental health. It is not practical to be all things to all and be there and here for everyone at the same time. I soon learnt that sometimes I will have to disappoint some people to protect my sanity and for a healthier relationship in the end. The key is to do it with empathy and grace. Now, when someone says to me, *"Sorry, I can't make it,"* even if I feel a little disappointed, I understand that we need to do what we must to look after ourselves and be better parents to our children.

VI – Being 'authoritative' rather than 'authoritarian' or 'permissive'

Under normal circumstances, parents should have some authority and control over the children. However, in today's society, with some broken homes and with the parents perhaps dealing with some personal issues, we find that children can get out of control, or even worse, they control the parents. Either end of the spectrum is not ideal as there should be a healthy balance between parents guiding their children and allowing them to discover themselves.

The 1960s developmental psychologist Diana Baumrind from the University of California found that there are three kinds of parents:

- Permissive parents try to be non-punitive and accepting of the child's mistakes without correction
- Authoritarian parents try to control the child based on a set standard of conduct
- Authoritative parents direct their child rationally

Generally, the acceptable (albeit old-fashioned) style of parenting appears to be authoritative, whereby the child grows up with a respect for authority but does not feel stifled by it.

SUMMARY: PARENTS' ATTRIBUTES

- Parents are critical to the well-being and success of their children
- Some of the key attributes that parents who raise successful children have in common are:

  1. High expectations
  2. Healthy relationship between the parents
  3. Higher educational levels
  4. Good time management
  5. The mothers work
  6. They're authoritative

CHAPTER 9

Mind-set and Values

"Teach them to your children and to their children after them."
Deuteronomy 4:9 (NIV)

Great leaders are not born ready to go; their experiences, exposure, abilities developed from challenges, shape them to become leaders. Disappointments, failures and learning how to handle challenges are part of the formula – for the course of life.

As parents, strong managerial skills to plan, organise and coordinate running a successful home are necessary, along with the leadership qualities to inspire and motivate our children. However, we can only do our best and feel reassured in the fact that we have given our children the best platform and start we can based on the information available to us to help steer them to their purpose. This book is a useful toolkit to complement what you're already doing and to increase your awareness.

To put things in perspective, let me share the story of Michael Fuller, whom I met at a talk. All things being equal and going by the findings of some of the research from leading institutions explored in this book, you would expect that Fuller would have turned out to be a failure. According to the statistics, Fuller, who was transferred from one foster carer to another, and possibly exposed to the worst parts of society, would have been expected to end up a criminal on drugs or may not have even survived his teenage years. Ironically, it turned out quite the opposite. Defying all odds, Fuller ascended to a leading position in the Kent police force and became one of the first chief constables from an ethnic minority background in 2004. By the time Fuller retired, crime had reduced by 22% in his jurisdiction and he had won several awards for his leadership skills. Under his leadership, Kent was highlighted by Her Majesty's police inspectorate as having one of the most improved police forces within England and Wales. Fuller believes everyone has a fair opportunity to create a positive change in society. Despite his humble beginnings and limited parental nurturing, he overcame setbacks and adversity as he rose through the ranks to the top of the police service as a chief constable.

The point is that there are examples of people who become a success without the nurturing described in this book. However, we shouldn't just leave things to luck and chance if we are able to nurture our children to be better and to maximise their potential. It is about ensuring they develop the right mindset, values and behaviours that will sustain them through life.

Let me share some insights I gained while participating in a leadership development programme at Harvard University, from a guest lecturer, Henry D. Wolfe, an activist investor. Activist investors tend to invest in companies that they believe could do better with some tweaks, such as a leadership change. As an exercise, Henry asked the class to brainstorm the one criterion he uses to decide on a CEO. The class got together in groups to brainstorm to determine what this single deciding attribute could be. Some suggestions were confidence, expertise, gravitas, humility, charm, authority, etc. However, it turned out that the one overarching criteria Henry used to determine how effective and successful a CEO would be was their mind-set. In decision theory, a mind-set is a set of assumptions, methods or notations held by one or groups of people. A mind-set also describes a person's philosophy of life. In the following section of this book, I discuss how, as parents, we can create the right culture and environment to help our children develop the right mind-set: a growth mind-set.

1 – Growth mind-set and valuing effort over avoiding failure

World-renowned Stanford University psychologist Carol Dweck explains that success is not just down to our abilities and talent. It is down to whether we have a 'fixed' or 'growth' mind-set. Therefore, with the right mind-set, we can motivate our children and help them to perform well in school, as well as reach our own personal or professional goals. The two types of mind-sets are defined as follows.

A fixed mind-set assumes that our character, intelligence and creative ability are fixed, such that we cannot change in any meaningful way and success is because of inherent intelligence. With a fixed mind-set we believe that failures define us and we are more likely to make statements such as, *"I'm no good at dancing!"*

However, someone with a growth mind-set thrives on challenge and sees it as a springboard for growth and stretching existing abilities. With a growth mind-set, weaknesses are seen as a challenge that can be overcome, with statements such as, *"I can't swim yet, but if I focus and practise, I can learn to swim."*

According to Dweck, when children are praised about their performance on a task because of their natural ability, this creates a fixed mind-set. However, if they are told that the success on a task is because of focus, effort and determination, this leads to a growth mind-set. Therefore, not only is it important for parents to develop a growth mind-set, but it is critical that we help our children do the same.

Children are generally eager to learn when the passion for learning has been nurtured over time. Meghan shares that her six-year-old daughter is aware of the Growth and Fixed mind-set concept. She explains that these are the sort of concepts that are taught early in schools with more resources. She goes on to explain her family's curated ecosystem – how the whole environment is encouraging the potential that the child can achieve – from observing their parents working hard and juggling the day-to-day.

Sometimes the flipside of having children develop all the skills discussed in this book is that they may become out of touch with some in society who may not be consciously developing the same life skills. The concepts explored in this book require a balancing act and have been positioned to help parents see their blind spots, to enable them to help their children round off better – by focusing on soft skills to complement the hard academic skills learnt at school.

II – Values-driven framework

Some of our greatest learning opportunities come from what people don't do for us. According to Christensen, learning to solve our own problems helps us to develop character and empathy, which leads to healthy self-esteem and confidence.

Pivoting on this point about learning from doing, the more we outsource our role as a parent, the more we lose the ability to help shape our children's value system. If our children gain their values and priorities from other people, whose children are they? It is also not practical to spend every waking moment with our children. The key is to be strategic and ensure we are at least present at critical moments to demonstrate the right values. What is at risk when we outsource? Our values, our culture, what we do and do not do, and why.

Although our children may not necessarily be ready to learn at the same time we want to teach them, there is great value in exposing children to experiences before they need them in order to prepare them. As stated before, children learn more from what they observe. We should be proactive about teaching them, while also learning to discern the moments they are ready to learn. However, to mitigate missing their cue, we should strive to consistently display through our speech and conduct, the values we want our children to learn, showing kindness, respect for differences and empathy. It is important also that, when children are ready to learn, it is not someone else with the wrong value system teaching them.

Over the years there have been several myths about raising children. For example, the myth of natural goodness identified by author William Kilpatrick in his book *Why Johnny Can't Tell Right from Wrong*. This idea suggests that virtue will take care of itself if children are just allowed to develop in their own way and create their own values. But what chance do they really have to do so when the rest of society, from scriptwriters to celebrities, advertisers, entertainers, and influencers insist on imposing their values on our children. Does it make sense for parents to just be neutral bystanders?

There has been so much emphasis placed on the unique, creative and unplanned nature of children, that parents have come to feel they need to adjust themselves to their children, rather than children learning to adjust to the requirements of family life. The reality is that a healthy balance is necessary and there are certain principles and values we should follow and teach our children, if we want our family to be blessed.

The overarching attribute that the young leaders from the focus group, Mark and Rose, highlighted was good values. They believe that a sound values-based mind-set is critical, as success is only worthwhile and a source of pride if you make a difference to society and change someone's world for the better. When you help and mentor others you increase your leverage, says Mark, as the people you help can reach people you cannot. Mark says finding someone a job is one of his greatest achievements, as it means he has changed the world for someone in a way that may create a ripple effect in their community.

By the end of the interview, I came to learn that Mark, an Oxonian PhD scholar and a high-flying management consultant, still does not feel like he has achieved much. At first, it seems when a child is pushed too far there is the danger that they develop an insatiable desire to overachieve. However, when I probed deeper, Mark explains that he cannot take credit for his achievements as it has been a collaborative and collective effort. He shares and triangulates what he defines as his secret weapons (see figure 6). The first is genetics, which contributed to his innate ability that he didn't have any control over, some might call it luck, or gifted. The second is values, instilled by his parents. Third is resilience, from his personal discipline and drive to achieve. Mark states that society sometimes measures success in the wrong way – instead of academic results, it should be about the value added to society.

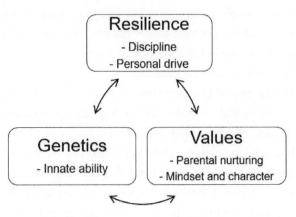

Figure 6: M's Triangle of Success

Mark concludes that he gets more satisfaction out of mentoring and helping people, which creates a ripple effect of opportunities propagated from helping one person.

SUMMARY:
MIND-SET AND VALUES

1. Nurture a growth mind-set
2. Instil values and a sense of purpose

CHAPTER 10

Future Proofing

"Do not follow where the path may lead. Go instead where there is no path and leave a trail."

Ralph Waldo Emerson

The industrial revolution required muscle from its workers. The information age traded muscle for mental capacity. The future will require workers to be emotionally intelligent, as discussed extensively in Chapter 1: Hard Skills versus Soft Skills. We are now in the fourth industrial revolution (4IR), which has led to advanced robotics, early trials of autonomous transport, artificial intelligence (AI) and machine learning. The fact is that some jobs will disappear by the end of the decade, whereas others that do not exist today will become the norm. In order to thrive in this new age, we must all upgrade our skillsets. The future of work belongs to those who possess emotional and social skills; therefore, we must prioritise these skills as part of our children's development in order for them to be future proof.

In the AI-driven world of tomorrow, where technology can diagnose a patient's condition with greater accuracy than a human doctor and do much of the heavy lifting, while the technical hard skills of doctors will remain important, their emotional intelligence will take on new significance and become more valuable.

The age of AI is fundamentally shifting the skills required to be successful. Over time, we have strived to make things better, faster and cheaper. It appears that every iteration of automation brings us closer to human redundancy or replacement. The increasing prevalence of AI and automation will make some traditional jobs and skills obsolete. In order to be future proof, three key skills that will be most sought after by 2030, according to a report by McKinsey Global Institute, are:

1. Technological skills
2. Social and emotional skills
3. Higher cognitive skills

Most importantly, technological skills (which can be derived from creative thinking) embrace everything from basic to advanced IT skills, data analysis, engineering and research. These skills are likely to be the most highly rewarded as companies seek more software developers, engineers, robotics and scientific experts.

Secondly, social and emotional, also known as soft skills, which is the focus of this book, include advanced communication and negotiation, empathy, the ability to learn continuously, to manage others and to be adaptable. Business development, programming, emergency responses and counselling require these skills.

Lastly, higher cognitive skills, which include advanced literacy and writing, quantitative and statistical skills, critical thinking, creativity and complex information-processing skills, will still be very relevant. Doctors, accountants, research analysts, writers and editors typically use these skills.

The report's authors add that:

> "Demand for higher cognitive skills such as creativity, critical thinking, decision making and complex information processing may grow through 2030 at cumulative double-digit rates. The growing need for creativity is seen in many activities, including developing high-quality marketing strategies. The rise in complex information processing, meanwhile, is related to the need to be aware of market trends and the regulatory environment that affects a company's operation, or the need to understand and explain to customers the technical details of a company's products and services."

The McKinsey report predicts that demand for higher cognitive skills in the US in 2030 may rise 9% and 7% for Western Europe. However, the call for soft skills (social and emotional) may rise by 26%. Critically, workers with technological skills, by 2030, may experience the biggest proportional increase in the demand for their time: a rise of up to 60%.

Sometimes I reflect on the sort of technology accessible today compared to what was available when I was in secondary school about 25 years ago. The level of advancement has been astronomical; I can only imagine how advanced technology will be in 25 years' time. Let me share a story about the evolution of seedless grapes to help illustrate this point. In the summer of 2018, I noticed the grapes bought for the week were still in the fridge, barely touched. Usually the grapes would only last a couple of days. When I decided to help myself to some, my daughter exclaimed, *"Mummy, don't eat those; they've gone off. Something is wrong with them!"* When I asked why she thought that the grapes had gone off, the reply was a revelation. *"There are seeds in them because they have gone off. Grapes don't normally have seeds."* At this point it dawned on me that for the last ten years or so, with the increasing availability of seedless fruits, it seems I have only ever bought seedless grapes. On this occasion, it appears that somehow, through online grocery shopping, I had mistakenly ordered seeded grapes or perhaps they were substituted. However, quite worrying for my husband and me was the fact that we were raising a generation of 'seedless grape' children, who may be missing out on gaining a balanced perspective. Although knowing that grapes can be seeded or seedless is hardly groundbreaking, this however highlighted a gap in knowledge and understanding.

From a quick cursory research, I learnt that in most grocery stores today the only types of grapes you can buy are seedless, due to the evolution and enhancement across all grapevines in production. Most fruits today come from cuttings rather than seeds, although scientists are still working on citrus fruits. The branch cuttings are dipped in rooting hormone and then placed in moist dirt for roots and leaves to form. Essentially the vines are clones of the vines they were cut from. Seedless grapes actually do contain seeds at some point. However, a genetic error as part of the process prevents the seeds from forming hard outer coats like those found on normal seeds. This incident made me wonder whether there was a missed opportunity for our children, from understanding from first principles about how some things have evolved over time. For example, what do we consider normal today that will look 'off' to children in the future? With the increasing technological disruption through artificial intelligence and robotics – with driverless cars imminent on our streets – I wonder if one day, seeing someone driving behind the wheel of a car may look 'off'. More critically, as parents, how do we ensure our children (and ourselves) will be prepared for a future that will operate very differently to what we understand to be normal today? Although, according to the below quote, the future is unlikely to arrive one day at a time, just as it has always done.

> "The future is already here – it is just not very evenly distributed."
>
> W Gibson

This quotation challenges me and begs the question, do we really need to prepare for the future? Especially if it is already here for some. The reality is that the traditional type of jobs known to be the safe jobs may change and no longer be as safe sooner than we expect. In my generation, traditional safe career paths were medicine, accountancy, law, engineering and perhaps teaching. I learnt about the investment banking sector while at university. Not many people are aware of the disruptive new sectors and industries being created over time under our noses every day. For example, I recently heard that AI is starting to disrupt the writing industry, with robots being used to write some fictional stories. With such blind spots, parents are therefore more likely to guide their children towards something they know. Starting my career in an investment bank opened up opportunities for me in other industries, such as the insurance sector and asset and wealth management sector, which I never knew existed. This is the reason I continue to do more research about artificial intelligence and robotics, and how they will not only shape our children's future but ours. Will robots become our masters or slaves?

According to *Forbes*, three of the five core skills of the future include: flexibility and adaptability, data literacy, and tech savviness.

I – Flexibility and adaptability

There are increasingly fewer and fewer skills and jobs for life. Therefore, everyone will need to be flexible and adaptable, being prepared to update their skills every few years and accept new ways of doing things.

II – Data literacy

Data is the fuel of the fourth industrial revolution that we're experiencing today. However, the data explosion is only worthwhile when people have the data skills to extract insights and make better decisions based on the data. Essentially, a case of how effectively data can be monetised.

III – Tech savviness

The fourth industrial revolution is bringing together a lot of major technology trends that are not only transforming businesses but reshaping our world.

Some of the jobs around today at the time of writing may likely not exist in five to ten years. With the continuing explosion of AI and robotics, this may continue to evolve the workplace too. How do we ensure that our children are positioned to take advantage of the opportunities that will be available? Better still, rather than waiting for the future to happen, how do we enable our children to be one of the architects to assemble the future, starting today? Thinking ten to 20 years ahead, we could be anticipating the problems of tomorrow and starting to think about the solutions.

A leadership culture

"If your actions inspire others to dream more, learn more, do more, and become more, you are a leader."

John Quincy Adams

The best practices covered in this book require active engagement with our children on a daily basis. Diplomacy may not always be appropriate as we assert the defined and agreed culture. As parents we may need to 'fight', though not literally, to maintain discipline, focus and encourage situations that bring the family together, driving away any distractions, negative and disruptive influences. Enduring and loving relationships with our family are worth fighting for. Be astute and protect against all the exposure to the dark side of social media. Be vigilant and discerning. There are two ways of fighting – you can choose the strategic or reactive route. For example, with the strategic route, you might plan where you want to live and what schools you want your children to attend in advance, to ensure they are exposed to the right influences. In the event that this is not practical, you have to be vigilant to ensure your children are self-aware, situationally conscious and have open discussions about why they should choose a certain path, and choose carefully. This means being comfortable with temporarily falling out as you correct an undesirable character trait. This can be challenging. There are times when, even if it hurts, you need to provide honest feedback; tell your children the truth kindly, but also be there to provide comfort as they come to terms with that and make the desired change. As parents, it may sometimes feel like you are in a constant battle to fight off distractions and negative influences seeking out your children. This is not a physical fight or act of violence; it is a spiritual fight, it is a mental fight and it could sometimes be counter-cultural. But fight you do, by defining your values and boundaries for the family, while remaining open to seek wise counsel as necessary.

Defining your family culture

One year around October, after observing that some priorities had slipped, we convened a family meeting with our children, who were seven and nine years old at the time. The purpose of the meeting was to discuss the state of affairs, receive and give feedback on how to resolve recurring issues, and how we wanted to describe the culture we're nurturing. Collectively, we decided that 'order' would be one of the concepts to cultivate in our small family unit. As part of the process, a number of illustrations were used to articulate the expectations, such as if any of us saw anything out of place on the floor we would restore order and put it in the right place. We also agreed to be up and ready by 6.30 a.m. daily to read, pray, or complete some light chores, etc. Of course, it took time for that to embed and on some days we failed miserably. The key was to try again the next day, keep going, and amongst ourselves we reinforced the expectations through reminding each other. If someone did or said something out of order, we would all call out 'order.' This was humorous at times, but slowly and surely we were weaving *order* into our family culture. Some benefits became evident with time and others are yet to materialise.

Embedding a leadership culture

Culture, formed over time through repetition, can be a blessing if the right priorities are proactively designed into it. Let me use a story to illustrate this point. In the early 1990s, Pixar was known as the leading technological pioneer in the field of computer animation. *Harvard Business Review* reported how Pixar fostered a culture of excellence. They did this by setting up a forum to receive feedback on a daily basis from anyone at any level within the organisation, with the aim of creating great rather than mediocre films. According to Ed Catmull, president of Pixar and Disney Animation Studios, by rejecting mediocrity at great pain and personal sacrifice, Pixar made a loud statement that it was unacceptable to produce some good films and some mediocre films. This mind-set of excellence became deeply ingrained in Pixar's culture, and it was constantly reiterated that everything they created had to be excellent. This goes beyond the movies themselves, to the DVD production and extras, and to the toys and other consumer products associated with the characters from the Pixar movies.

A good takeaway here is to define a culture of values and priorities in your home to enable children to make decisions independently. Children should also understand there are consequences to unwise decisions, and the need to take responsibility for their actions or inactions. It requires a conscious effort to build and reinforce the desired culture, otherwise getting away with things with no consequences and bad behaviour may start to become the culture.

Culture is formed through everyday interactions and once set, it becomes almost impossible to change. The marginal cost of deviating and doing something just once may appear negligible at first, but the full cost is much bigger in the end. Drawing on my professional experience, for example, for most of the big banks that failed during the global financial crisis of 2008, the root cause can be traced to a small action or error thought to be negligible initially but festered until it was too late to rectify. The same principle works with the little naughty things our children do that we overlook: the little talkback, the tiny bite, the small tantrum, that small white lie, or teensy disobedience. These actions, albeit negligible at first, when left unchecked, accumulate and could lead to disaster and issues in adulthood. Small lies accumulate into bigger lies.

Some people are driven by achievement, and in the worst cases some start cutting corners just so they can continue to be seen as a success and an achiever. It starts with that first step and the next one seems relatively smaller. Before they know it they are further down that slippery slope than they intended – thus the peril of marginal thinking, according to Clayton Christensen. Marginal thinking is an economic theory that requires decision-makers to evaluate whether the benefit of one more unit of something is greater than its cost. However, the bright side is that the same principle can work the other way. The small good deeds and everyday choices could lead to the desired outcome in the end, when applied consistently.

After you have done the best you can and applied the best practices you can find, the overarching advice will be to continue to pray according to your religious beliefs or hope for the best outcomes for your children in everything. Although, prayers can act as an insurance hedge over and above all our efforts and best practices. Ultimately, children are a gift from God with their unique paths and destiny, and our role as parents is to support and enable them to maximise their potential and make the world a better place.

The entire essence of this book can be summarised as follows – in order to ensure your child maximises their potential and lives a happy and fulfilled life, as parents it is wise to plan ahead, ensuring the right building blocks of the foundation are put in place early on. Put another way, if you want your child to go to a leading university one day to study, you need to plan for it. In some cases it may happen naturally. However, in most cases you need a strategy – how to increase your chances and make it happen. It will take discipline and hard work to create the opportunity. The key is to choose what works best for your family situation and work towards your goals in the best way you can.

> "Teach them to your children and to their children after them."
>
> Deuteronomy 4:9 (NIV)

Leaders Never Stop Learning

"As we look ahead into the next century, leaders will be those who empower others."

Bill Gates

I came from and married into a family with strong values. As I advance in years, though the composition evolves, my 'villagers' are all contributing to both the person I am today and will become tomorrow. I'm passionate about learning and I proactively seek out opportunities to develop spiritually, personally and professionally. I have learnt and continue to learn a lot from my family, spiritual leaders, mentors, friends, colleagues, acquaintances and Biblical scriptures to discover my purpose, why God created me. Therefore, I try not to leave my purpose to chance, and I am deliberate in the pursuit of my purpose. I am currently a Financial Services Risk and Strategy professional, property developer, author and speaker, using my expertise to make a living. At the same time I have a passion to make a positive difference in people's lives and add value to our society, summarised by this quotation from Mother Teresa:

> "I alone cannot change the world, but I can cast a stone across the water to create many ripples."

Acknowledgements

Nurturing Soft Skills is very much a collective effort. I believe it was God-inspired when I was expecting my first child, and when I came across the work of Jean Piaget, the Swiss philosopher. My desire to be the best parent I can be and subsequent search for best practices set in motion a lot of the thinking that led to this book. Thank you, God.

My husband, CJ Ani, has always been a source of inspiration and support. His critique of the earlier drafts of the manuscript has resulted in *Nurturing Soft Skills* covering a broader range of topics, most notably, the financial literacy section. Thank you, dear.

Interactions with spiritual leaders, mentors, colleagues, ex-colleagues, friends and mentees have directly and indirectly contributed to making *Nurturing Soft Skills* much better as a result. Pastors Matthew and Yemisi Ashimolowo, my spiritual parents, for the spiritual foundation, teachings on the importance of meaningful names, and property ownership alluded to in Chapter 7, Mr Bimbo Odunsi and family, Mrs Ade D'Almeida for discovering my speaker potential and giving me my first speaking opportunity in 2004, Dr Dipo Oluyomi and family, Mr Gbenga Fashanu and family, Mr Dayo Ogundayo and family, GB-Dumaka family, Mr Soji Otudeko and family, Mr Obi and Mrs Eva Nwosa and family, Mrs Jenny Francis my first mentor, Mrs Melissa Charleton my first manager, Mrs Sarah Murray and family, Mr Mark Allan FIA, Mr Gilbert Gbedawo and family, Mrs Teresa Esan, MBE for the various speaking opportunities over the years, Mrs Yana Wilson, Mrs Rachel Oliver, Mrs Naomi Agyekum and family, Mr David and Mrs Jacinta Klutse and family, Mrs Bess Obarotimi and family, Dr Melvin Mezue, Mr Henry D. Wolfe, activist investor and author of *Governance Arbitrage* for the Harvard guest lecture on the CEO mind-set. I am also grateful to Mr Jim McLaughlin my executive classmate at Oxford University for his input in me arriving at the title of the book. I have been fortunate to have Paul Roberts edit the final draft of the book. His feedback has led to a more polished output.

I was also inspired by the work of author Malcolm Gladwell, namely the bestseller *Outliers*. Clayton Christensen, former Harvard Business School professor and author of *How Will You Measure Your Life?*, was also a source of great inspiration.

I owe thanks most of all to my early family – the Osalors and the Johnsons, my grandparents Chief George and Mrs Eunice Osalor, Mr Marlborough and Mrs Mary Johnson, my parents, Mr Peter FCA, CTA, and Mrs Eudora Osalor, my brothers Daniel and Victor and their spouses Shyama Osalor (nee Broady) and Abi Wheeler (Osalor) respectively, my big aunt and uncle Dr Moses and barrister Gogo-Rose Ilo, my uncle Mr Harold Johnson (Engr.) for teaching me lots of Christmas carols and how to play chess, and my uncle and aunt Dr Hashim and Mrs Stella Gibrill for always travelling around the world to seek out family members. I'm thankful to my parents-in-law Mr Henry (Engr.) and Dr Glory Ani and, the rest of my in-laws, Chief Murphy and Mrs Kanayo Aro-Eneh, Mr Nnamdi and Dr Ginika Ilechukwu, and Mr Zuby Ani and Dr Uju Zoe Ani (nee GB-Dumaka) for their family orientation and values. This is a book about parents making an effort to the best of their knowledge to give their children the best start in life. I learnt the importance of integrity, excellence and diligence from my parents and grandparents. My father is very ambitious and hardworking; he tackles work with enthusiasm and innovative thinking. This entrepreneurial flair, which he learnt from his mother, my grandmother, who raised me in my early years, is evident in everything he does. My mother taught me how to communicate with more diplomacy and the importance of preserving relationships; both my mother and grandmother taught me the beauty in soft answers, although this is still a work in progress. I did not know it growing up, but my parents, grandparents, aunts and uncles helped to shape my firm foundation by demonstrating the importance of family. My children, to whom *Nurturing Soft Skills* is dedicated, have given me a new lease of life, the priceless gift of love and the opportunity to learn and become a better person. Life continues to be a perpetual learning process.

Thank God and, to all of you, thank you.

Additional Resources

This section offers general guidelines to help parents understand what to expect from their child at different ages. As normal, you should discuss any concerns you may have about your child's development with their doctor or teacher.

As an additional resource, Child Prodigy, a child development programme, offers workshops using the COACH framework.

1. Stages and expectations in child development

Age	Expectations
Four years	Having mastered the basic concepts in life, your child will now enter the exciting stage of learning how to apply and build on them. In the year up to their fourth birthday: • Children make a huge transition, moving from parallel play to a much more interactive form of play with others. • When engaging in role-playing with other children, your child will learn about cooperation and sharing, and this is an important way for pre-schoolers to attempt to understand the adult world. • Play also affords children the opportunity to act out their feelings.
Five years	At five years, your child might start school. • Adjusting to life in reception and Year One, learning to sit still and concentrating for longer periods of time will be some of the biggest accomplishments. • Five-year-olds typically understand and apply concepts such as under, over, because, why, before and after. • Your child will not only be writing the letters of the alphabet but will probably also be identifying the sounds that correspond with many of them. Reading is a skill that a handful of children excel in and the vast majority start to learn only when they go to school.
Six years	• Your child is now ready to start Year Two. • They will probably be thriving on new friendships, working out what makes the world tick and becoming independent. • Your child may begin to lose their baby teeth between five and six years of age, soon to be replaced by their permanent teeth. • Your six-year-old is probably getting better at reading and may even be reading simple chapter books.
Seven years	• Your child may be reluctant to try out new activities, preferring the familiar, and might have trouble concentrating at school. • Your child may start writing joined up using full stops, commas, capital letters and question marks correctly. • They may understand the difference between fact and fiction as well as how riddles, rhymes and tongue twisters work.

Age	Expectations
Eight years	• Eight-year-olds enjoy having the opportunity to solve problems independently. • They are able to concentrate on tasks for longer periods and begin to use their own resources prior to seeking adult help or they may seek out peers for assistance. • Eight-year-olds demonstrate more highly developed thinking skills, as well as the ability to solve problems with creative strategies.
Nine years	• Children are at a major development transition. • In many ways, nine-year-olds are still young children, but they are becoming much more independent and are developmentally mature enough to handle many responsibilities. They are increasingly expanding their social circles to include more people outside of their parents. At the same time, nine-year-old children still need and want a secure relationship with their parents, and follow their parents' example.
Ten years	• When children hit the double digits, many of them think they are almost teenagers. • While some ten-year-olds start looking and acting more grown-up, others stay more child-like – physically, emotionally and socially. • Having a strong sense of self and confidence can be very important at this age. • When children have strong and healthy self-esteem, they will be better equipped to handle any potential pressure from peers who might try to convince them to do things they do not feel are safe, healthy or morally right.
Eleven years	• Your child's growing independence from the family and interest in friends might be obvious by now. • Healthy friendships are very important to your child's development, but peer pressure can become strong during this time. • Children who feel good about themselves are more able to resist negative peer pressure and make better choices for themselves. • This is an important time for children to gain a sense of responsibility along with their growing independence. • Another big change children start to prepare for during this time is starting secondary school.

Source: Adapted by author from various sources

2. Gifted children – a checklist for parents

The below checklist was developed by Mensa, the society for bright people, to help parents identify whether they have a gifted child.

A gifted child may display some or many of these behaviours.

Behavioural traits	Y/N
An unusual memory	
Passing intellectual milestones early	
Reading early	
Unusual hobbies or interests or an in-depth knowledge of certain subjects	
Intolerance of other children	
An awareness of world events	
Set themselves impossibly high standards	
A high achiever	
Prefers to spend time with adults or in solitary pursuits	
Loves to talk	
Asks questions all the time	
Learns easily	
Developed sense of humour	
Musical	
Likes to be in control	
Makes up additional rules for games	
Extrovert/introvert	

3. Managing the holidays

The holidays can sometimes be a challenge for parents, whether you work full time or not. I am sharing some tips from other parents on how they keep children entertained over the holidays when at home:

1. Drawing up a weekly lunch menu
2. Story writing
3. Swimming lessons
4. Help with laundry
5. Word searches

The below table sets out different age-appropriate responsibilities:

Age	Responsibilities
Pre-schoolers	• Set the table. • Wipe out sink after brushing teeth. • Turn off all the lights when family is leaving the house. • Feed a pet. • Tidy up his/her room.
Age 6–11	• Carry clothing to laundry room and sort. Put away clothing after it is clean. • Load dishwasher. • Vacuum a room. • Organise his/her closet. • Help make dinner (older kids can graduate to doing this on their own). • Pack own lunch and make own breakfast. • Help purchase/create thank-you gifts for teachers, babysitter, etc. • Do something nice for someone who is experiencing sickness or loss. • Clean out the back seat of car. • Be responsible for homework. • Use phone to call grandparents, friends, etc. • Order for herself/himself at restaurants. • Have own library card and be responsible for late fees.

Source: A Fine Parent, by Cara Sue Achterberg.

Balance is important and where possible parents should take the children away on holiday.

4. About Child Prodigy

Child Prodigy was founded in 2009; it is a private UK company. The founders are entrepreneurs with professional backgrounds in financial services and IT consultancy, who are also parents with extensive experience of child development. The founders have a combined 35 years' working in the city within some of the most prestigious and global leading institutions.

From the founders' combined experiences, they have defined the following core principles that underpin the Child Prodigy vision and framework:

- **C**onfident – *confidence leads to better performance*
- **O**utgoing – *charisma and likeability are fundamental to absolute success as they open doors and attract favour*
- **A**rticulate – *better communicators generally excel*
- **C**reative – *creativity and innovation are critical to sustainable success*
- **H**appy – *a great attitude is essential as people generally like people with a great attitude.*

The framework has proved effective for developing these key soft and leadership skills in children.

Development of the Child Prodigy programme

A series of 30 pilot Child Prodigy workshops were conducted in 2014, attracting positive feedback and testimonials from the parents and children who took part.

After the pilot ended, a number of parents enquired about further connecting with the material, and asked that I provide a book. After some reflection, I decided it would be useful to share the material with a wider audience, particularly given that the resources to run workshops in numerous locations are somewhat limited. The Child Prodigy programme uses the framework discussed in this book to set the agenda for the holiday workshops. This has been tried and tested and it works – as can be judged from the testimonials from parents. This programme material has been developed and refined over a 12-year period. The material in this book further supports the information already held by the pilot workshop participants, while also reaching a wider audience of parents who may want this information to apply from home.

What to expect

Whether it is in front of the class or on stage, it is important for children to be engaged in activities that exercise the skills for confidence, problem solving, creative thinking, motivation, teamwork and so on to maximise their potential. Child Prodigy workshops provide structured, fun-based activities incorporating the skills discussed in this book.

The underlying fundamental is forging a strong

connection between the soft skills children learn outside of school and time spent in the classroom, integrating non-cognitive skills into a cognitive-based skill sets.

The workshops have been designed in consultation with professionals including teachers, child development psychologists and childcare professionals. They are delivered by qualified practitioners/teachers.

To register your interest for our summer holiday workshop go to www.childprodigy.org.uk

Child Prodigy Apps

The following Child Prodigy apps are available to download for free on the App Store and are compatible with iPhone, iPad, and iPod touch.

1. Maths
2. Child Education – Preschool and Reception

ChildProdigy Education	ChildProdigy Maths
Description: educational games for pre-school and reception age children. Age 3 - 5. Contents include learning the alphabets, counting, colours, shapes, fruits, animals, body parts, vehicles, months of the year and days of the week.	Description: basic arithmetic. Age 5 – 8. Your child can practise and master addition, subtraction, multiplication, division for the infant level to juniors. Beginning from level 1, higher levels automatically unlock as your child progresses.
Link to download - https://apps.apple.com/us/app/childeducation/id1086108025	Link to download - https://apps.apple.com/us/app/childprodigymaths/id1086157299

Workshops

Child Prodigy runs a full week of workshops focussed on developing these key skills during the summer holidays. To register your interest go to www.childprodigy.org.uk

Reference Notes

Introduction
Beckett, A. (2017) 'PPE: the Oxford degree that runs Britain', https://www.theguardian.com/education/2017/feb/23/ppe-oxford-university-degree-that-rules-britain

Cullinane, C., Montacute, R. (2017) 'Improving essential life skills for young people', https://www.suttontrust.com/wp-content/uploads/2017/10/Life-Lessons-Report_FINAL.pdf

NASA (2011), 'The law of aerodynamics according to NASA', https://www.nasa.gov/audience/forstudents/k-4/stories/nasa-knows/what-is-aerodynamics-k4.html

Chapter 1: Hard Skills versus Soft Skills
Bradberry, Travis (2014) 'Emotional Intelligence – EQ', https://www.forbes.com/sites/travisbradberry/2014/01/09/emotional-intelligence/

Bradberry, T. (2015) 'Powerful Ways to Mold Your Children into Leaders', https://www.forbes.com/sites/travisbradberry/2015/08/11/8-powerful-ways-to-mold-your-children-into-leaders/#634004ea4ff4

Carter, Carol J. (2013) 'How Soft Skills, Passion and Connection Can Promote Learning, Competence and Employability', The Huffington Post, October 21, http://www.huffingtonpost.com/carol-j-carter/how-soft-skills-passion-c_b_4124034.html

Gladwell, M. (2009) Outliers: The Story of Success, Penguin

Goleman, D. (1996) *Emotional Intelligence*, Bloomsbury

Jenkins, R. (2019) '*This Is the Most In-Demand Skill of the Future*', https://www.inc.com/ryan-jenkins/this-is-most-in-demand-skill-of-future.html

Marr, B. (2019), '*The 5 Most Important Job Skills for the Future*', https://www.forbes.com/sites/bernardmarr/2019/11/04/the-5-most-important-job-skills-for-the-future/#5c6b1ad71e5d

Maxwell, John C. (2012) *Failing Forward: Turning Mistakes Into Stepping Stones for Success*, Thomas Nelson Publishing, first published 2000

McGonigal, Jane (2010) '*Gaming can make a better world*', https://www.ted.com/talks/jane_mcgonigal_gaming_can_make_a_better_world

Phillips, L. (2012) *The Artistic Edge: 7 Skills Children Need to Succeed in an Increasingly Right Brain World*

Skillicorn, N. (2016) '*Leaders agree: Creativity will be 3rd most important work skill by 2020*', https://www.ideatovalue.com/inno/nickskillicorn/2016/09/leaders-agree-creativity-will-3rd-important-work-skill-2020/

TalentSmart (2019) '*WORLD'S #1 PROVIDER OF EMOTIONAL INTELLIGENCE*', http://www.talentsmart.com/about/talentsmart.php

Chapter 2: Confident

Achterberg, C. S. (2015) '*Are You Teaching Kids Responsibility? 50 Simple Challenges to Get You Started*', https://afineparent.com/building-character/teaching-kids-responsibility.html

Baumrind, D. (2003) '*Effects of authoritative parental control on child behaviour*', http://persweb.wabash.edu/facstaff/hortonr/articles%20for%20class/baumrind.pdf

Duncan, Greg J. et al. (2007) '*School readiness and later achievement*', *Developmental psychology* vol. 43, 6, 1428–1446, https://www.ncbi.nlm.nih.gov/pubmed/18020822

Gillett, R., Premack, R. (2015) '*Science says parents of successful kids have these 11 things in common*', https://www.businessinsider.com/how-parents-set-their-kids-up-for-success-2015-11?r=US&IR=T#they-teach-their-kids-social-skills-2

Leopold, W. (2007) '*Early academic skills, not behaviour, best predict school success*', https://www.northwestern.edu/newscenter/stories/2007/11/duncan.html

Sabolava, K. (2020) '*Birth order impact on personalities*', https://www.independent.co.uk/life-style/health-and-families/oldest-sibling-leadership-natural-younger-middle-child-a9334696.html

Sutton, M. (2017) *'Birth order may affect sibling career prospects'*, https://www.goodhousekeeping.com/uk/news/a568159/middle-children-more-li, kely-to-be-ceo/

Weller, C. (2015) *'The single best thing parents can do to make sure their kids are successful'*, http://uk.businessinsider.com/the-most-important-thing-for-kids-to-be-successful-2015-11?r=US&IR=T

Chapter 3: Outgoing

Burns, J. (2013) *'Talking at mealtimes boosts children's confidence'*, https://www.bbc.co.uk/news/education-23502947

Donnelly, L. (2019) *'Children spend twice as long on smartphones as talking to parents'*, https://www.telegraph.co.uk/news/2019/02/07/children-spend-twice-long-smartphones-talking-parents/

Gillett, R. (2015) *'Research says this is what you need to teach your kids in kindergarten if you ever want them to go to college or get a job'*, http://uk.businessinsider.com/future-success-could-be-determined-early-2015-7?r=US&IR=T#ixzz3hCRlz0Oc

National Literacy Trust (2012) *'Family mealtime chat'*, http://www.wordsforlife.org.uk/family-mealtime-chat

Chapter 4: Articulate

Gilbert, L. (2014) *'A Brief History of Henry Hoover'*, https://www.ransomspares.co.uk/blog/news/a-brief-history-of-henry-hoover.htm

Kuper, S. (2018) *'Why three is the magic number'*, https://www.ft.com/content/30ef660e-076c-11e2-92b5-00144feabdc0

Mrs Wordsmith, *'10,000 word journey'*, https://www.mrswordsmith.com

Chapter 5: Creative

Hull, R. PhD (2016) *'The Art of Nonverbal Communication in Practice'*, https://journals.lww.com/thehearingjournal/Fulltext/2016/05000/The_Art_of_Nonverbal_Communication_in_Practice.5.aspx, *The Hearing Journal*: May 2016, Volume 69, Issue 5, p. 22, 24

Internet Matters (2018) *'How can parents counter the narrative and encourage 'critical thinking' when it comes to protecting children against extremist influences (on and offline)?'*, https://www.internetmatters.org/hub/question/how-can-i-help-my-child-to-think-critically-to-protect-them-against-extremist-influences/

Ofcom (2007) *'The UK Children's TV Market'*, https://www.ofcom.org.uk/__data/assets/pdf_file/0024/33675/market.pdf

Strauss, V. (2013) *'Top 10 skills children learn from the arts'*, https://www.washingtonpost.com/news/answer-sheet/wp/2013/01/22/top-10-skills-children-learn-from-the-arts/?utm_term=.20eae284a47d

Chapter 6: Happy

Barker, J. (2011) *'How to Raise Healthy Children: It's a Family Affair'*, https://www.webmd.com/parenting/features/raising-healthy-children#1

Cooper, C. (2015), *'Overly-controlling parents cause their children lifelong psychological damage, says study'*, http://www.independent.co.uk/life-style/health-and-families/overly-controlling-parents-cause-their-children-lifelong-psychological-damage-says-study-10485172.html.

Jordan, L. (2018) *'6 Things That Make Children Feel Loved'*, Psychology Today

LiveScience (2012) *'Typical Toddler Behavior, or ADHD? 10 Ways to Tell'*, http://www.livescience.com/22362-adhd-symptoms-guide.html

Lythcott-Haims, J. (2015) *How to Raise an Adult*, Bluebird

Nierenberg, C. (2013) *'Regular Bedtime For Kids Could Be The Secret To Good Behavior'*, http://www.huffingtonpost.com/2013/10/14/kids-bedtime-behavior_n_4096675.html

O'Shea, E. (2018), *'Common mistakes parents make'*, https://www.netmums.com/child/common-discipline-mistakes-we-all-make

Packham, A. (2019) *'Here's why you should walk your child to school'*, https://www.huffingtonpost.co.uk/entry/walk-children-to-school_uk_5d848c9ae4b0849d47271bd8?guccounter=1&guce_referrer=aHR0cHM6Ly93d3cuZ29vZ2xlLmNvLnVrLw&guce_referrer_sig=AQAAADt2BfTLu8i5qj7uXEDhaBFqkdQV1IrloHpiCh6D63bWcANn1kwUEmyxkpDTQDC71MTs72XnsUp6Od4QiqG8oPAy78ACkXi3NkSddBZa_C5jT_QUV1TDNdLmehPML4zpwHzi0L2teiaIQXLjmDpd007APIo4TpU9kzWPvGLMKHzA

Pappas, S. and Peterson, E. (2016) *'25 Scientific Tips For Raising Happy (& Healthy) Kids'*, https://www.livescience.com/17894-10-scientific-parenting-tips.html

Paruthi, S., Brooks, L. J., and D'Ambrosio, C. (2016) *'Recommended Amount of Sleep for Pediatric Populations'*, https://www.ncbi.nlm.nih.gov/pubmed/?term=D%27Ambrosio%20C%5BAuthor%5D&cauthor=true&cauthor_uid=27250809

Pearson, H. (2011) *'Epidemiology: Study of a Lifetime'*, https://www.nature.com/news/2011/110301/full/4710209.html

Rees, C. (2007) *'Childhood attachment'*, Journal of General Practice, https://www.ncbi.nlm.nih.gov/pmc/articles/PMC2169321/, 2007 Nov 1, 57(544): 920–922.

Stafford, M., Kuh, D. L., Gale, C. R., Mishra, G., and Richards, M. (2015) '*Parent–child relationships and offspring's positive mental wellbeing from adolescence to early older age*', Journal of Positive Psychology, 11 (3) pp. 326–337, http://discovery.ucl.ac.uk/1476806/

Zelman, K. (2020) MPH, RD, LD, '*The My Plate Guide to Healthy Eating*', https://www.webmd.com/vitamins-and-supplements/nutrition-vitamins-11/quick-tip-my-plate

Chapter 7: Financial Intelligence Quotient (FiQ)

Clear, J. (2020) '*40 years of Stanford research found that people with this one quality are more likely to succeed*', https://jamesclear.com/delayed-gratification

Collinson, P. (2017) '*We will all pay the price for financial illiteracy*', https://www.theguardian.com/money/2017/may/27/financial-illiteracy-young-people-oecd-study

The Money Charity (2016) '*Financial education in schools: how to fix two lost years?*', http://themoneycharity.org.uk/financial_education_schools/

OECD (2017) '*Launch: OECD PISA financial literacy assessment of students*', http://www.oecd.org/daf/fin/financial-education/launch-pisa-financial-literacy-students-2017.htm

Springer, S. (2013) '*Many money habits are set by age 7*', www.mtmfc.org/many-money-habits-are-set-by-age-7/

Whitbread, A. and Brigham, S. (2013), *Money Habits are Set by Age 7*

Chapter 8: Parental Attributes

Brettig, K. (2015) '*The Children Communities Connections learning Network, Building Stronger Communities with Children and Families*', https://www.cambridgescholars.com/download/sample/62450

Burkeman, O. (2016) '*Why time management is ruining our lives*', https://www.theguardian.com/technology/2016/dec/22/why-time-management-is-ruining-our-lives

Carter, S. B. (2012) '*Emotions Are Contagious—Choose Your Company Wisely*', https://www.psychologytoday.com/blog/high-octane-women/201210/emotions-are-contagious-choose-your-company-wisely

Centers for Disease Control and Prevention, Division of Human Development and Disabilities (2020) '*Middle Childhood (9–11 years of age)*', https://www.cdc.gov/ncbddd/childdevelopment/positiveparenting/middle2.html

Christensen, C. (2012) *How Will You Measure Your Life?*, Harper Business

Christou, L. (2017) 'CEO baby names: These are most popular rich and powerful names of the year', https://www.verdict.co.uk/ceo-baby-names/

Dean, J. (2015) 'This Early Parental Behaviour Predicts A Child's Academic and Social Skills 3 Decades Later', http://www.spring.org.uk/2015/01/this-early-parental-behaviour-predicts-a-childs-academic-and-social-skills-3-decades-later.php

Dubow, E. F., Boxer, P. and Huesmann, L. R. (2020) 'Long-term Effects of Parents' Education on Children's Educational and Occupational Success: Mediation by Family Interactions, Child Aggression, and Teenage Aspirations', https://www.ncbi.nlm.nih.gov/pmc/articles/PMC2853053/

Duckworth, A. L., Peterson, C., Matthews, M. D., and Kelly, D. R. (2007) 'Grit: Perseverance and passion for long-term goals', Journal of Personality and Social Psychology, 92(6), 1087–1101, http://psycnet.apa.org/record/2007-07951-009

Duncan, Greg J. et al. (2007) 'School readiness and later achievement', Developmental psychology vol. 43, 6, 1428–1446, https://www.ncbi.nlm.nih.gov/pubmed/18020822

Dweck, C. (2014) 'Fixed vs. Growth: The Two Basic Mindsets That Shape Our Lives', https://www.brainpickings.org/index.php/2014/01/29/carol-dweck-mindset/

Gillett, R. and Baer, D. (2015) 'Science says parents of successful kids have these things in common', http://uk.businessinsider.com/study-working-mothers-and-career-success-2015-5?r=US&IR=T#ixzz3hCLfRLd0

Hector (2017) 'How Titans Manage Time: Warren Buffett and Free Time', https://focusme.com/blog/how-titans-manage-time-warren-buffett/

Hughes, R. Jr., PhD (2005) 'The Effects of Divorce on Children', https://www.ideals.illinois.edu/bitstream/handle/2142/14470/The%20Effects%20of%20Divorce%20on%20Children--2005.pdf?sequence=2

Larson, K., Russ, S. A., Nelson, B. B., Olson, L. M., and Halfon, N. (2015) 'Cognitive Ability at Kindergarten Entry and Socioeconomic Status', http://pediatrics.aappublications.org/content/135/2/e440

Lee, K. (2017) 'Child Development Milestones of Your 9-Year-Old Boy or Girl', https://www.verywell.com/child-development-nine-year-old-620731

Murphy Paul, A. (2013) 'What We Expect From Ourselves And Others Often Becomes Reality', http://www.businessinsider.com/set-high-expectations-for-yourself-and-others-2013-3?IR=T

Nauert, R., PhD (2015) 'For Some Parents, Kids Are College-Bound From Day One', https://psychcentral.com/news/2015/01/26/parental-expectations-influence-childrens-academic-success/80420.html

Ninh, A. (2011) 'Does Your Name Spell Power? LinkedIn Reveals Top CEO Names', http://newsfeed.time.com/2011/04/28/does-your-name-spell-power-linkedin-reveals-top-ceo-names/

Pink, D. (2012) 'How to predict a student's SAT score: Look at the parents' tax return', http://www.danpink.com/2012/02/how-to-predict-a-students-sat-score-look-at-the-parents-tax-return/

Raby, K. L., Roisman, G. I., Fraley, C. R., and Simpson, J. A. (2014) 'The Enduring Predictive Significance of Early Maternal Sensitivity: Social and Academic Competence Through Age 32 Years', http://onlinelibrary.wiley.com/doi/10.1111/cdev.12325/abstract

Rieman, M. (2012) 'Top 10: Most Popular CEO Names', https://www.nerdwallet.com/blog/investing/top-10-popular-ceo-names/

Robert Wood Johnson Foundation (2015) 'Children With Strong Social Skills in Kindergarten More Likely to Thrive as Adults', https://www.rwjf.org/en/library/articles-and-news/2015/07/new-research--children-with-strong-social-skills-in-kindergarten.html

Schulte, B. (2015) 'Quality time trumps quantity', https://www.washingtonpost.com/local/making-time-for-kids-study-says-quality-trumps-quantity/2015/03/28/10813192-d378-11e4-8fce-3941fc548f1c_story.html?utm_term=.0d5ef44984ce

Spickernell, S. and Ehrenberg, B. (2015) 'These are the UK's most popular chief executive names', http://www.cityam.com/222470/these-are-uks-most-popular-ceo-names

Sugar, R. (2015) 'Harvard researchers find working mothers have more successful daughters and conscientious sons', http://uk.businessinsider.com/study-working-mothers-and-career-success-2015-5?r=US&IR=T#ixzz3hCLfRLd0

Tang, S. Davis-Kean, P. E., Chen, M., Sexton, H. R. (2014) 'Adolescent Pregnancy's Intergenerational Effects: Does an Adolescent Mother's Education Have Consequences for Her Children's Achievement?', http://onlinelibrary.wiley.com/doi/10.1111/jora.12182/abstract

Noble, C. (2015) 'Kids Benefit From Having a Working Mom', https://hbswk.hbs.edu/item/kids-benefit-from-having-a-working-mom

Chapter 9: Mind-set and Values

Dweck, C. (2017) Mindset: changing the way you think to fulfill your potential, Robinson

Wolfe, H. (2014) 'Corporate governance lecture', Harvard University

Chapter 10: Future proof

Jenkins, R. (2019), '*This Is the Most In-Demand Skill of the Future*', https://www.inc.com/ryan-jenkins/this-is-most-in-demand-skill-of-future.html

Ventresca, M. (2019) '*Innovation Strategy Lecture*', Said Business School, Oxford University

Wagner, T. (2014) *Creating Innovators: The Making of Young People Who Will Change the World*, Simon & Schuster Children's Publishing

Conclusion

Catmull, E. (2008) '*How Pixar Fosters Collective Creativity*', https://store.hbr.org/product/how-pixar-fosters-collective-creativity/R0809D